TOO MUCH INFORMATION?

TOO MUCH INFORMATION?

Ten essential questions for digital Christians

Andrew Graystone

CANTERBURY
PRESS
Norwich

© Andrew Graystone 2019

First published in 2019 by the Canterbury Press Norwich
Editorial office
3rd Floor, Invicta House
108–114 Golden Lane
London EC1Y 0TG, UK
www.canterburypress.co.uk

Canterbury Press is an imprint of Hymns Ancient & Modern Ltd
(a registered charity)
Hymns Ancient & Modern® is a registered trademark of

Hymns Ancient & Modern Ltd
13a Hellesdon Park Road
Norwich
Norfolk NR6 5DR, UK

British Library Cataloguing in Publication data

A catalogue record for this book is available
from the British Library

978-1-78622-159-9

Typeset by Mary Matthews

Printed and bound in Great Britain by
CPI Group (UK) Ltd

Contents

Acknowledgements   vii
Introduction   ix

1   Are Machines Getting Smarter – Or Are
    Humans Getting More Stupid?   1
2   Where Am I?   15
3   What is Happening to My World?   30
4   Who Owns My Information?   46
5   What's the Difference Between a Person
    and a Machine?   70
6   Who is My Digital Neighbour?   91
7   Who Am I These Days?   105
8   Who Can I Believe?   122
9   Is it Time to CTRL+ALT+DELETE
    the Church?   138
10 Is My Body Due for an Upgrade?   157

What Next?   178
Glossary   186

Acknowledgements

I'm grateful to the Sir Halley Stewart Trust and the Seedbed Trust, and to the many friends and family who continue to support my quirky vocation.

Nine times out of ten, when I have had a thought about life in digital culture, I discover that Dr Bex Lewis has had it first. Among all the naysayers she is relentlessly positive about the possibilities of technology and of life itself. She will disagree with some of what I have written here, especially my use of the term Real Life. ('But, Andrew, it's *all* Real Life.') She is right of course. If anyone knows about Real Life, it is Bex. This book is dedicated to her.

Introduction

In 1543 Nicolaus Copernicus published his work *On the Revolutions of the Heavenly Spheres*. His radical idea was that we humans are not at the centre of the universe but that, like other planets, our earth orbits the sun. He was right of course. But his discovery didn't just prompt the rewriting of the relevant pages in the astronomical texts of the day. Adjusting to this new piece of information required an agonizing mind-shift for the entire human species. It took at least 200 years for the culture to adjust to the news that we were not at the centre of things.

Open a map on your phone or your laptop today, and a little pulsing blue circle will tell you where you are. Wherever you are in actual space, the blue circle on the map will be right at the centre. Copernicus' long-fought battle to convince his fellow humans that they existed on the edges of a much wider galaxy has been thrown into reverse. Once again digital culture is telling us that the universe revolves around us. Only this time it isn't the planet that's at the centre, but every individual.

You will notice that I'm talking about digital culture here, not digital technology. I'm not primarily here to discuss how the Church can make best use of new digital communications media … whether bishops should blog or how churches can use the web. Those things are important, but they are not the heart of our conversations here. If you need someone to help you set up a website or choose which phone to buy, you've come to the wrong person. In fact I think those questions are relatively trivial, and if that's what you need to know you would probably be best to ask a teenager for help. For me, what is fundamentally important is not digital technology and what we can do with it, but digital culture and what it will do to us. What forces are shaping the digital environment? How is the Internet changing our understanding of ourselves as individuals and communities? What is happening to authority? What does it mean to be a disciple in a digital age? It is these bigger questions that pose the greater challenges to Christians, and those are the sort of questions we will deal with in this book.

> What is important is not digital technology and what we can do with it, but digital culture and what it will do to us.

The rise of digital culture has had an unsettling effect on Western humans just as great as the Copernican revolution. The root of this disquiet is the sense that the place of human beings in the cosmos has shifted fundamentally. Until the middle of the twentieth century, we were sure that the human brain was the most powerful tool we had available for processing information. We could confidently live as if we were the centre of the universe of information. For all its weaknesses and unreliability, we assumed that the body, made up of flesh and blood, atoms and molecules, arms and legs and brain, was the basic unit of humanity. The body was the only place where we had power or agency. Digital culture calls these fundamental assumptions into question.

Way back in 1985 the writer Neil Postman wrote a prescient book about media culture, which he called *Amusing Ourselves to Death*. In it, he complained that media culture pitches us into 'a neighborhood of strangers and pointless quantity; a world of fragments and discontinuities'.

The advent of digital media has transformed our access to information and made new forms of relationship possible. It has also increased exponentially the pointless quantity and discontinuity that Postman warned about.

Today we live with the uneasy feeling that all the important stuff is going on elsewhere, where data is being sifted by machines. If we stop to think about it, we know that those machines must themselves be located somewhere, in some physical space. But it doesn't feel like that. It feels as if information about us and our lives is being stored and processed in some sort of ephemeral realm outside of space and time. We are aware of its complexity, the power and the richness of the activity going on there, but we quite literally can't get our hands on it. Some of the words we use add to this sense of unreality. 'Cyberspace' is a metaphor that tries to envisage the digital environment as akin to physical space – except that you can't locate it, measure it or visit it. We store information in 'The Cloud' – another metaphor for something that we know is real but fluffy, intangible and beyond our control.

Everyday instances of automation add to this sense of detachment. A mechanical voice answers the phone or tells us where the bus will stop next. A letter arrives from the bank that has clearly been generated by a computer. A website posing as a friend recommends a book or offers a discounted holiday. After a few weeks of living in a digital culture we are well aware that these people who *seem* to be speaking to us are not *actually* speaking to us. Or rather, they are speaking, but they are not actually people. They are signals generated by an algorithm, which have never passed through human lips. After a few months we stop being surprised or disappointed that the communications aren't genuine. Wisdom teaches us to be cynical about emails bearing gifts. After years of digital exposure we hardly notice that most of the people who seem to be communicating with us aren't real at all. We know that there was a person attached to the voice once, or at least that somebody has made decisions to program the message. But the actual people behind the communication barely exist to us in any real way. They are more part of the machine than of our community.

Digital information is non-physical. And because our cultures generally adjust themselves to meet the limitations and requirements of the new technologies available to them, digital culture has downgraded the physical. That includes the status of the human body. Later in this book I will have lots to say about what it means to be human in digital culture. Much of it is exciting – but some of it is disturbing too.

> Digital culture has downgraded the physical.

We are once again at the dawn of a new age in human culture (or more accurately, we are at around half past nine in the morning of the new age). The tool that has brought this about is the Internet. Its forms and uses are every bit as diverse as the hammer, and its impact on human culture promises to be just as great. Billions of fingers are touching, tapping and swiping billions of screens to access almost immeasurable amounts of computing power. But in a strange kind of judo-throw the computer is also acting on us, and on the people we know, and on the whole of human culture. The changes we are seeing are probably bigger and more fundamental in scope than anything we have seen in a hundred human lifetimes, but like gradual changes in the climate they are hard to notice and respond to. Since the challenges of the digital age affect the most fundamental of beliefs, such as what it means to be a human, you might have thought that Christians would be at the forefront of exploring them. Unfortunately we are still mostly busy trying to remember our passwords and work out how to set up a church Facebook page. My aim in this book is to explore some of the ways that digital culture is affecting us. I don't claim to have big enough answers even for my own questions, but we need to identify the challenges so that we can make measured decisions about how we want to live in this first digital age.

The digital era crept up on me. One minute I was looking for a phone box to call home, and a copper 2p coin to pay for the call. The next minute I was carrying a phone in my pocket and paying the bill with a credit card using money that never existed except as numbers in my bank's computer. Like most of us, I was so busy focusing on the practical issues – what sort of computer shall I buy; should I give my child their own phone – that I didn't stop to think much about the bigger issues. To be fair, in the earlier days of broadcasting these were issues that had been dealt with by someone else. No-one was keeping a record of what TV shows I watched or who I phoned and for how long. (No-one, except possibly my mother.) Now, though, like the media itself, the issues seem to have come much closer to home.

Do I have a right to keep my personal data private, and if so, how can I do that when every shop seems to want to know my name, address and shoe size before they will serve me? If I write a blog or take a photo and put it online, is it still mine? Is anyone else entitled to change it, share it and even make money out of it? Then there's the tricky balance between freedom of speech and prevention of harm: does the government have a right and duty to check what I'm writing in my emails if they believe that by doing so they might stop someone attacking our country? Can (and should) children and vulnerable adults be protected from violent or pornographic images and ideas that are so easily accessible online?

These are all part of a broader question about what it means to live well in a digital environment. I have discussed them with Christians all over the world. In their responses they tend to fall into two groups. About half of my audiences react as if digital culture is bringing about the most profound, challenging, exciting opportunities of our age, and it is a privilege to be alive at this time. Wouldn't St Paul have loved to live in the twenty-first century, they say? He would have been podcasting his sermons and Skyping his distant congregations. We would be studying Paul's 364th email to the Corinthians. The chaos of the Tower of Babel is reversed, as the whole world finally speaks in one language – a language made up of endless sequences of 1s and 0s. The other half of my listeners tend to screw up their eyes and ears, in the hope that they can just about get through to retirement before they have to think too hard about all of this! You

Some people believe that this is the moment when humankind passes its sell-by date.

won't be surprised to know that I fall into the first group, though I share many of the misgivings of the second group, as new technologies break over our heads like waves crashing onto a sea wall. This is an extraordinary moment in the development of humankind. Some people, as you will read, genuinely believe that this is the moment when humankind passes its sell-by date. I don't agree with them. But I do believe this is a hinge point in history, and a make or break point for the Christian community. To live well in a digital age we will need to ask ourselves some extremely challenging questions. So let's start.

1

Are Machines Getting Smarter – Or Are Humans Getting More Stupid?

The magic touch

When I was 11 years old, I went to visit my father in the 26-storey modernist office block in Central London where he worked. The only thing I remember about the day is the lifts. I was allowed to summon the lift by touching a square button that instantly lit up to say the carriage was on the way. I'd been in lifts before of course; in the department stores my mum sometimes took me to to buy school clothes. In those lifts there was a round Bakelite button that stood out from the wall and moved under your finger with a satisfying clunk. This lift was different. The button wasn't a button at all, but a square shape with round corners, etched on the lift wall. This square was touch sensitive. Nothing moved. It simply reacted to the heat of an enthralled 11-year-old finger. I think. The science-fiction writer Arthur C. Clark said: 'Any sufficiently advanced technology is indistinguishable from magic.' Summoning a lift from 26 floors up using just the power of my finger felt like a kind of wizardry.

You may be reading these words on the inked pages of a book made out of a recycled dead tree. But you may equally well be reading the letters formed of the absences of light on a tablet computer, or even on a pocket-friendly smart phone with a touchscreen. If so, you may be curious as to how the screen takes instructions from your finger and turns them into actions. There are several possibilities, but the most common is that, beneath the transparent protective layer that cracks so easily, there is a thin film carrying a grid of hundreds of thousands of minute capacitors. When you touch the screen a tiny electrical charge is transferred to your finger. The voltage drops minutely in the part of the screen you are touching, as the current flows to earth through your body. That's why you can't operate a touchscreen with gloves on, but you can operate it with a raw sausage. Try it.

Your fingers are probably so big that they touch scores of capacitors at any one moment, but the particular combination of switches tells the device at which point on the grid the current has dropped. It sends an instruction through the device's processor, and causes it to perform a particular function, say, open an application or phone a friend. Scientists developing the very earliest touchscreens in the 1970s held a series of meetings to agree a common 'language', so that tapping the screen, swiping it from side to side, 'pinching' or even stroking it with multiple fingers sends an instruction that the device can understand. Of course, to manage such detailed instructions from such a vast range of possible choices the processors have to be enormously powerful. The processing power in an average smart phone is greater than the processing power that was available to NASA in the 1960s to send human beings to the moon.

At one level this is fantastically clever. To have conceived of this possibility, and worked out how to engineer it at such a microscopic level of detail; to create a business model that allowed the devices to be made in huge quantities for an affordable price; to develop applications that have transformed the way we bank, shop, play games and communicate with people around the world – our generation has been blessed with a string of developers for whom the word genius hardly seems adequate. And (provided you can afford it) you can access all of this technology and control it with the touch of your forefinger.

Of course touch-screen technology is nowhere near its zenith yet. New techniques are developing all the time. In the next few years we'll see screens you can fold up like a handkerchief and put in your pocket, screens used as architectural material in buildings, and screens that have a sensitivity to pressure, warmth and position as well as just the touch of your finger. Amazing.

> Touch-screen technology is nowhere near its zenith yet.

And that finger ... how exactly does *that* work?

Well, it has no muscles at all. That's right - the ultra-fine motion control that your fingers are capable of is generated by muscles in your palm and forearm, not your finger itself. They are connected to tendons that provide an amazing degree of motion control. The skin on your fingertip has several layers and embedded in them are millions of receptors that respond to stimulation. Thermoreceptors enable your skin to sense heat; nociceptors allow you to feel pain; and four different types of mechanoreceptors respond to various pressure, vibrations and stretching of the skin. In fact there are more receptors in your fingertips than anywhere else in your body except your genitals. Compartmentalized pads of fat act as shock absorbers. They are packed with capillaries less than 10 micrometres in diameter making your fingers ultra-sensitive. Nerve cells communicate with each other by secreting molecules that transmit signals to your brain at a speed of about 170 miles per hour. Each finger relates to a distinct area of your brain where the signals are processed, evaluated and co-ordinated, so as well as being interchangeable for some tasks, they can work in concert (literally, if you are a musician). Further instructions may be transmitted from your brain through your nerves and back to your muscles at around 250 miles per hour resulting in movement or other responses. Professor Mark Rutland of the Royal Institute of Technology in Stockholm has discovered that a human finger can feel a bump corresponding to the size of a single molecule. That enables us to discriminate between surfaces that are flat and those that have ridges as small as 13 nanometres high. By comparison, if your finger was the size of the whole earth, it would be sensitive enough for you to feel the difference between houses and cars. It would, however, be a nightmare finding gloves to fit.

A finger is pretty amazing. It is the place where your mind meets the world. You can use it to touch, point or play the violin. It is a dual-purpose tool for exploring and also controlling your environment. It is so well adapted that nine times out of ten you can touch something and understand it, even when you can't see it. You can even fix your hair with your eyes closed. Wearing gloves if necessary.

As I said, the finger is pretty amazing. And you are provided with not one, but ten of these devices, cunningly located in groups of five on each arm. Even more remarkably, two of your fingers have been adapted into thumbs. They are opposable, meaning that they are capable of meeting your other fingers tip to tip in a pincer movement. This incredibly useful feature is shared only with the higher apes. Sir Isaac Newton once said: 'In the absence of any other proof, the thumb alone would convince me of God's existence.' And he had two of them. Your fingers are also mounted on a fully flexible wrist that gives them almost infinite mobility. The surface cells are ready for action six months before your birth and are renewed every month of your life.

Our brains have become adapted so that they notice tiny movements of another person's fingers across a huge distance, as any orchestral conductor can tell you. Can you imagine what happens when the fingers of one person touch the fingers of another?

> Human to human touch is the most intense and powerful exchange of information yet discovered.

I do hope so. Human to human touch is the most intense and powerful exchange of information yet discovered. Opposable thumbs mean that human beings can lock hands in a way that is unknown anywhere else in the animal kingdom.

By comparison with your finger, the touchscreen on your phone is rather limited. It can only sense where your finger is – not how hard it is pressing, whether it is wet or dry, how warm it is, what it feels like, what shape it is … Its language is limited to taps and swipes. Put your finger to your lips and a tablet computer won't realize that you want it to be quiet. Point at an object and a smart phone won't turn to look. A computer essentially does what it's told – what it has been programmed to do. A finger, on the other hand, can take initiative.

When a finger touches a screen – or for that matter a keyboard or any other form of controller – something remarkable and yet remarkably ordinary is happening. In a sense a computer is no more than a sophisticated man-made tool. It is an accessory to enhance human activity, just as a pair of spectacles or a hearing aid are enhancements. It is a logical extension of the development of the hammer (though you are not recommended to knock nails in with an iPhone). The genius, the wonder and the majesty are all on the side of the finger, not the computer.

As you use your phone or computer, you are aware that you are one of 15 billion people who have occupied the planet over millions of years. You may also be conscious that there are more than 4 billion other people who at this very moment are potentially connected to you through the Internet. Your computer, on the other hand, is blissfully unaware that there are any other computers apart from itself. It is innocent of its own existence. It is oblivious to the fact that by connecting to the Internet it effectively becomes just a tiny part of a vast computer that contains more gathered information than the world has previously known. It doesn't even know you're there. It is a machine. You are a person.

> Your computer is blissfully unaware that there are any other computers.

Tools change us

You might think that means that all the action is one way – that your finger is the do-er and shaper of events. But you'd only be partly right. When we use tools of any kind – a hammer, an egg whisk or an iPhone – we are trying to shape the world around us in some way. We use a tool because it allows us to extend our own powers, to hit harder, whisk faster or call further than we could without it. But no technology is neutral. As we use tools to shape the world, they in turn shape us. And we in turn are forced to respond to the transformation by changing ourselves. Every piece of equipment we use or invent makes new things possible and old things impossible. It has its own impact on us; on the way we see ourselves and the ways we live together. Whether or not we choose to engage with it, technology changes us.

The invention of the hammer, for instance, made it possible to build bigger and better shelters to live in. It also made it possible to knock down your neighbour's shelter if it was in your way. And *in extremis*, it made it possible to knock down your neighbour. The person with the biggest hammer quickly realized that he had more clout than the person with the biggest muscles. So it became important to make a bigger hammer and grow bigger muscles to wield it with – and thus began the arms race. The person who invented the hammer only intended to use it to build a better shelter, but its very existence changed his perception of himself and his neighbour.

> As we use tools to shape the world, they in turn shape us.

It wasn't all good, and it wasn't all bad. The hammer itself turned out to be pretty much a morally neutral object. But a new age of human civilization had dawned, based around the existence of the hammer. Call it Hammer Time.

The American cultural theorist Marshall McLuhan is credited with describing the transformational impact of every new technology on the nature of human relationships. When we use tools of any kind, he said, we are engaging in an imaginative process to shape the world around us. But technology is not neutral. As we use tools to shape the world, we are in turn forced to respond to the transformation by changing ourselves. The technology makes its own impact. We don't have to be passive in this. We have choices to make. But if we don't make the choices – if we allow technological advances to carve out their own path like a river running down a hillside, then we and future generations will have to live with the consequences of the choices we failed to make.

That's why an Internet iconoclast like Jaron Lanier is so useful. He is a computer scientist of the first rank, who pioneered the notion of virtual reality (and invented the term). He has developed cutting-edge techniques for medical imaging using computers. But he questions the orthodoxy

Future generations will have to live with the consequences of the choices we failed to make.

that computers are getting smarter and smarter. Is it possible, he asks, that the machines we are making appear to be more and more 'intelligent' because humans are choosing to act more and more stupid? Have computers got smarter, or have people started to act stupid? When I type a request into a search engine it gives the appearance of knowing exactly what I want. But maybe I'm just adapting my expectations, degrading myself to make the computer seem clever. Lanier challenges the sci-fi assumption that information sources will necessarily aggregate and speed up until eventually a computer will be cleverer than a human brain. There is nothing clever or independent or free at all about the information a computer generates. No computer can or ever will have an independent existence because it takes at least one human person embedded in the culture to create the information and another to decode it. Otherwise it is meaningless.

So we have much more agency than we think. There are significant choices that we can make, and must make, about what it means to live well in the digital environment.

Jaron Lanier is a brilliant technologist but he is not a technological utopian. From his elevated viewpoint at the top of the digital mountain he gives a stark warning about the ways that technology is acting on us. He observes that when we are presented with a new technology we tend to diminish ourselves to accommodate to it. If all you have is a hammer, every problem looks like a nail. And if all you have is a computer, however big, every problem looks like a computation. 'Machines seem increasingly smart,' says Lanier, 'because humans are choosing to abase themselves in front of them.' Does Siri, or Alexa, or that annoying voice-

8

activated cinema ticket-booking service I phoned recently, really know the answers to the important questions I want answered? Or am I playing along ... playing dumb to make the machine seem clever?

Like so many of the issues that humans are facing in the digital era, this is not new. In the eighteenth century, in the period we call the Industrial Revolution, engineers began to develop machines that would vastly increase the rate at which goods could be produced and transported. Manufacturing moved from the workshop to the factory. In 1853 Richard Garrett and Sons of Suffolk developed 'The Long Shop', the world's first assembly line, where products (in their case steam boilers) moved through the factory on a railway line as various operations were carried out. The role of human beings was to operate the manufacturing equipment, and to do anything that a machine couldn't do. The trouble with this system is that if you are not careful you start treating human beings as just part of a big machine – an expensive part at that, and one that needs paying, is prone to breaking down, and sometimes throws a sicky on a Monday morning. One of the core values that Christians need to hang onto is that human beings are not machines. 'You are not a gadget,' as Jaron Lanier memorably says. Christians believe that humans have a unique status in creation. God did not create machines; God created humans, who went on to make machines. There's a big difference. God did not come to the earth as a machine; God came to the earth as a human being, with all the inconvenience and specificity that goes with that.

God did not come to the earth as a machine.

Digital culture has a strong tendency to underestimate the value and uniqueness of human beings; to treat them as just a rather inconvenient part of a much larger machine.

A great many discussions in this area focus on advances in digital technology – and of course they are dizzying. If you are anything like me, you are easily awed by clever technology. I've been to more than enough conferences where the speakers speculated on what technology will be available five, ten, fifty years from now. Sometimes they were proved right, and sometimes not. Often it felt as if the speakers were simply trying to bamboozle us or even frighten us with the imagined consequences. It is easy to be awed or frightened by technology. It used to be talking fridges and intelligent clothes. Now it is digital house elves and driverless cars and sex robots. In this book I'm only going to refer to technology that is already available. But in fact, it's not what's happening in technology that's fundamentally important, but what's happening in our culture.

Recently I went to the International Congress on Love and Sex with Robots (I went so that you didn't have to). It was full of academics talking about synthesized skin, virtual orgasms and teledildonics. The things I took away from it were: i) we can't agree on what we mean by a robot; ii) we don't know what we mean by sex; iii) no sex robots currently exist; iv) it's extremely unlikely that we will be able to create one; and v) if we did, we're pretty sure not many people would want one. But what was really important was not all the fascinating technology that is being built or imagined, but why so many people should consider having sex with a robot at all. We need to ask how living in a digital culture is changing us as people.

The infrastructure of life is increasingly autonomous – many decisions are now made not by an individual person but by a system that was programmed by a group of people we will never meet. When you search online for a restaurant near you the recommendation isn't made by a human, but by an algorithm – a little bit of computer program that has been designed like a mathematical equation to answer a question. Many financial decisions are not made by people but by algorithms; and I don't just mean city investments – it's more than possible that your application for a bank loan will be decided by an AI (Artificial Intelligence). Machine-generated legal and medical advice is already available; a trend that is likely to increase. And of course if you take a ride in a driverless car, it is algorithms that decide when the car turns, brakes and so on. We shop online, bank online, play, worship and talk to our grandchildren online. We use digital phones and send digital messages. Even my 85-year-old mother, who has never owned a computer herself, is known, remembered and processed by countless systems every day of which she is completely unaware.

In all these transactions we humans project ourselves into the world, in ways that are disembodied. We may have any number of disembodied representations (or *personae*), some of which we control, and some of which we're hardly even aware of. And my multiple projected personae may have all sorts of different characteristics that don't necessarily relate to the flesh and blood person who framed the words you are reading. It's the cultural impact of digital technology, rather than the technology itself, that we need to think carefully about.

Some people like to suggest that we're living through a 'digital revolution'. Personally, I don't think that language helps us. 'Revolution' suggests that everything has changed. It hasn't. It is just 30 years since the Internet became accessible to non-military users. A few months ago we passed a significant milestone, when for the first time more than half of the entire population of the world has access to the Internet. And although China and India are lagging behind, the prospect of the entire world being digitally connected can't be more than a decade or two away. Digital mobile phone coverage is even more ubiquitous. According to the International Telecommunication Union 4.1 billion people – around 60% of the world's population – now have a mobile phone contract. That's more people than have a flushing toilet. Digital language can store and convey almost any sort of information; text, images, sound and data. It is in effect a near-universal language, which transcends culture and geography. When even the self-consciously non-technical depend on digital information transfer, and technology significantly influences the shaping of culture, it is fair to say that we are living in a digital environment, a digital space, a digital age.

It is true that the introduction of digital technology has been hugely disruptive. It is true that the rate of change in digital technology has been dizzyingly fast. But for all that the rate of change is increasing, the impact of digital culture is essentially continuous with much of what went before. The rate may have changed – a digital hammer can strike harder by some orders of magnitude than an analogue hammer – but many fundamental things in digital culture are simply developments of what went before. People who were powerful in analogue culture are even more powerful in the digital era. People who were disadvantaged before are even more disadvantaged now, and so on.

People who were powerful in analogue culture are even more powerful in the digital era.

Even if this isn't a 'digital revolution' it is certain that we are in a period of massive change that will have an enormous impact on all our lives. Internet use is rising very sharply. The household computer has moved from the study to the living room to the pocket, as TV, radio, online games, telecoms and the web converge. The library of content available will soon be effectively infinite, with consumers downloading 'on demand' and paying for whatever they want, whenever they want it. In this environment everything from BBC1 to pornography starts on a level playing field.

One-directional media like TV and radio are struggling to retain their raison d'être as consumers choose media they can interact with. Look at the things we can do online already. We can meet, chat, shop, bank, worship, play, research, perform operations … We can play massive multi-player online games with strangers and friends anywhere in the world. We can form global online communities and even whole virtual worlds. We interact throughout the day and night over social networks like Facebook, Twitter and Instagram. Over the next ten years we're going to see an exponential rise in computing power that will have a profound impact on almost every area of our lives. A society that is

> We can form global online communities and even whole virtual worlds.

already soaked in digital media is about to be saturated. I'm convinced that this isn't just a change in technology – it is going to transform the nature of relationships and the way we communicate, it's going to change the way we think and the ways we understand truth.

During its adolescence the Internet has developed a strong set of principles, like the doctrines that take shape in the early years of the foundation of a new religion. For example, there is the principle that everything that *can* be available online, *should* be. Many people hold to these doctrines with the fundamentalist fervour of teenagers. For someone who isn't an expert in technology (and I certainly count myself in that group) it's tempting to be daunted by all of this. Dare I ask really fundamental questions about digital culture when half the time I can't make my own computer do the things I want it to? Will I be seen as a Luddite or a technophobe?

2
Where Am I?

The collapse of context

In the British Library near St Pancras Station in London there is a darkened room that displays original manuscripts from amazing works of music and literature. There are pages from the notebooks of the great artist and inventor Leonardo Da Vinci, all written with immense precision in his unique right-to-left mirror writing. You can tell from his handwriting that he had an incredible mathematical brain. In another case is the original manuscript for Handel's *Messiah*. It has obviously been written in a great rush – as if the composer is desperately trying to capture all this fantastic music and get it from his head onto paper before it flies away from him. And just a few feet away there's a cabinet full of Beatles manuscripts. There's the back of an envelope where Paul McCartney scribbled the words to 'Michelle'. There's a page torn from a notebook with the words of 'Yesterday' – his handwriting would never have got him through a school exam, but the words went on from that scrap of paper to become the most covered song of all time. And there's a large sheet of what looks like scrap paper on which John Lennon scribbled the words to 'Help'. It was scrawled out, practically in crayon. Listen to it, and you might think it's a jolly, bouncy pop song. But seeing it in Lennon's own handwriting you realize that the words were actually coming straight from the heart of a man who was feeling really desperate and alone. There's something immediate and personal about seeing words and music written in the authors' own handwriting. It tells you so much about them.

If Handel or The Beatles were writing their music today, they'd probably do it on a tablet computer. The text would be spell-checked and the font would be pre-set. The words might never make it onto paper at all. If they did, the layout wouldn't tell you anything about the person who wrote it or the moment the inspiration came.

Every act of communication, be it a song, a letter, a text or a tweet is about two human lives touching. That's why when I open the post in the morning I always look first for the ones with the handwritten envelopes. On my wedding anniversary I could send my wife a swift anniversary text, or maybe an email. But in the end, I choose a handwritten card, because I know she will be able to read far more into it than just the words I have written.

> Every act of communication is about two human lives touching.

One of the core features of digital transmission is the way it strips out the context from the information we send, receive and use. It's sometimes referred to as 'the collapse of context'. A book is a good example. You may be reading these words in the traditional form – that is, a lot of pieces of paper stuck together down one edge. If you have a book in your hands you aren't just holding the words and ideas I'm trying to convey. The book itself – the actual object – carries a lot of information that I never put there. There may be notes scribbled in the margins that will tell you someone else has read this book before you. There may be a mark where something was spilled on the page. You will have a sense, just from the object, as to whether this book is fairly new or very old. It may make you think of the time and place you bought it, or the person who gave it to you as a gift. Information held in a physical object like a book will change over time. The text will stay the same of course, but the object itself will accrue new information – a musty smell, yellowed pages or a cracked spine. In contrast, digital information is unaltered by time passing or distance travelled. If you are reading these words on a screen, they will look exactly the same every time you open the device. Digi-

Digital information comes without a context.

tal information comes without a context. It can travel across great distances and arrive in exactly the same condition in which it was sent. It can sit on a storage device for months or years, and when recalled it will appear exactly the same.

If I send an email to a friend in Australia it will take no longer to arrive than the email to a colleague on the next desk, and the contents will be entirely unaffected by the journey. This 'death of distance' contributes to what David Weinberger describes as 'the rise of the miscellaneous' and Ted Nelson calls the deep intertwingling of digital information. The trouble is, when context is lost, much of the significance and nuance of communication goes with it. All digital interaction has a tendency to strip out context. In his book *Lost Icons*, Rowan Williams asks: 'What happens to our sense of the human when it is divorced from a grasp of the self as something realized in *time*?' And if I were to give a bit of myself away, I would say that I think 'our sense of the human' is the thing we need to be most careful about as we step into the digital world.

Information that is stripped out of its context and 'miscellanized' is fun. It allows for multiple and randomized connections and a far richer possibility of inter-relationship. But it also poses questions about how we understand ourselves; the way the universe is ordered, and the significance of persons. The hierarchy of meanings we are used to living with is getting muddled up. Let me explain.

Imagine an object: let's say a football. You can pick it up and hold it. You can squeeze it, but only so far, because it has real substance. If you kick it hard, it will move away from you. Then maybe after a few seconds someone will kick it back to you. It's a solid, real, tangible object that occupies space and passes through time.

Now think about the word 'football', the word that describes that object. The word itself doesn't really exist in time. You can't pick it up and hold it or kick it. It describes the round object you were playing with a minute ago, but it isn't the same as that object. The word 'football' is not a football. You can't kick a word. It's just a label that conjures up an image of the object. You are pretty sure the football exists in real life, but it's harder to know in what sense the word 'football' actually exists. If I say the word out loud it exists for a moment as a bunch of sound waves and then it is gone. If I write 'football' on a piece of paper it exists as ink on a page – but even then, the word itself is not actually a football.

Don't worry if your head is starting to hurt. What really matters is that we agree that the word 'football' is not the same as an actual football. But in the digital environment all of that changes. Imagine a digital football. It might be flat on a screen or even a 3-D image floating in space like a hologram. It wouldn't weigh anything. It wouldn't take up any space. You couldn't touch it or kick it (which is a serious disadvantage if you want to play soccer with it). But you can certainly imagine it. In fact if you were clever with coding you could make it. A digital football could certainly exist. It just wouldn't exist in space and time.

That digital football you have created is actually just a sophisticated line of computer code. And that's where things get interesting. In the real world, a football is one thing, and the word 'football' is another. In a digital context there is no real difference between a thing and its label. Both exist only as a string of symbols. A digital representation of a football is not

> Expressing something in a digital form messes with the reality of it.

fundamentally different from the code that makes it up. The two levels of reality – the thing and its representation – are blurred. Expressing something in a digital form messes with the reality of it.

When we talk with someone face to face we're not only listening to the words they say. We're doing something much richer and more complex than that. We are hearing and interpreting the language they are using, our ears are picking up the physical vibrations that their voice-box is making in the air, and our brain is decoding those vibrations and turning them into sound. Then another part of our brain does a further decoding job and interprets those words, assigning them a series of meanings, then stringing the meanings together to make sentences and paragraphs that make a kind of sense. We're collecting and interpreting the words. That in itself is pretty clever. We have to work out what language the person is speaking in and check the meaning against the things we think they are likely to be saying, to see if we think what we're hearing is credible.

So when we listen to someone speaking, we're not just receiving and decoding their words. We are understanding them in a much wider context. We listen to the tone of voice – which gives us a whole lot more information about the meaning. Then we look at the expression on their face, and their body language, and that adds even more data to help us clarify the meaning. Even if you didn't understand the words – say because the person was speaking in a language you didn't know – you would still get a lot of helpful information from the look and sound of the person who was speaking to you. Microsecond by microsecond our brain is on the hunt for clues that help us to attach meaning to the interaction.

And there's more. As we listen to the person's voice and look at their face, we're also scanning the rest of the room. Is there someone approaching? What's behind the speaker? How far away are they standing? What other clues are there in the context to give us more information about what's being said? Are other people listening too? Are they laughing – or looking bored? What's the overall tone of the interaction? Is it a friendly gathering – or are we expecting a fight to break out at any moment? Second by second, we are making calculations about the nature of this conversation, judged not only by its content, but also by its context.

And there's more. Every conversation takes place in a wider context of what you might call history and geography. By history I mean the precise time when it happens – the date and month and year, and not only that, but also all that has gone before this moment and all that will come after it. And by geography, I mean the precise place where the meeting is happening. It might be in a school classroom, or halfway up a mountain. It might be in bed or while driving a car. It might be happening in Manchester or Melbourne or Michigan. All of this information adds layers of meaning to the encounter between two people. In fact we need to have most if not all of this information to make sense of the actual words. And within that complex mass of information we decide, either consciously or unconsciously, how we will react. Something inside us knows what faces to pull, what posture to adopt, and what words to say. We're unconscious experts at it.

Now imagine that instead of speaking to someone face to face you are connecting with them via a digital communications application like Skype. If you know the person, you will know a bit of their history. But the picture won't tell you precisely where they are. However detailed the image is, you won't pick up half of the visual clues as to what they are thinking and how they are feeling. You won't have any idea what they were doing ten minutes ago. The digital contact has enabled you to swap words and some feelings, but it has removed 99% of the context. If your contact is via a non-visual medium like email or text, even more of the context has been stripped out. That's why it is so easy to misunderstand what someone is saying to you by email, or to get the tone or the meaning wrong in a text message. If you're using a false name, or acting out your communication through an avatar, you will have even more capacity for confusing messages.

Actually, what has happened is not that there isn't a context. It's just that most of the context in terms of history and geography has been stripped out of the meeting, leaving a rather crude and limited set of signals for your brain to work with. It might be better than nothing if, say, it allows you to see pictures of your grandchildren in Australia. But it might equally be worse than nothing if it stops you from putting your arm around a close friend who is grieving.

Now, finally, imagine that instead of having a two-way conversation via a medium like Skype, your friend has simply recorded a message and put it up on YouTube. Now you don't even know where or when they said those things. You may not even be sure whether they were speaking to you or just sending out a message to the world. You can play the message

Watching a message on YouTube has about as much context as finding a message in an old bottle washed up on the beach.

again and again, but it won't carry any more meaning because the context is so limited. Watching a message on YouTube has about as much context as finding a message in an old bottle washed up on the beach. This 'collapse of context' that digital communication entails has undone what our ancestors took centuries trying to do, that is, to get things organized.

A major feature of the nineteenth century was the movement to classify information. There was a drive to identify chemical elements and put them into a periodic table. There was a race to name and catalogue all the species of flora and fauna, and to relate them to each other. And towards the end of the nineteenth century there was a movement to classify information, particularly the information that was contained in books held in libraries. The doyen of this initiative was a man called Melvil Dewey. Dewey was a strange character. He was an advocate of bracing winter sports, and a campaigner for the metric system of measurements. He was almost impossible to work with. He insisted that female applicants for jobs should include an intimate photograph of themselves with their application form, and he refused to employ anyone who was Jewish – or in fact religious at all. One biographer says of him, 'Although he did not lack friends, they were weary of coming to his defence, so endless a process it had become.' What Melvil Dewey *did* give us was the Dewey Decimal System – a method of classifying books into categories. As printing became cheaper and the mass-production of books was more common, some method was needed for organizing libraries. Simply having all the information in the head of the librarian wasn't working any more. So Dewey set out to list every subject about which a book might be written and give it a classification number. He tried to imagine every sort of information there could be and give it a three-digit number before the decimal point, relating to the broad subject area, with up to three numbers after the decimal point breaking the subject down again into more detail. Then if you needed more, you added the first three letters of the author's surname. In the Victorian era there were few enough books that the system worked really well. Every subject Dewey could imagine had a small section of its own.

Understandably, Dewey gave greater prominence to the subjects he knew most about. As time went on and knowledge developed, some of the categories didn't work so well any more. In the religion section, for instance (which is category 200 in the Dewey Decimal System), seven of the ten top-line numbers were devoted to Christianity. All the other religions in the world shared one 'other religions' number between them. Within that there was a separate sub-section for Judaism, and one for Zoroastrianism. But Islam had to share a sub-heading with Babaism and Bahai. That meant that Islam, Babaism and Bahai put together had the same prominence as parish administration, which had a sub-section of its own. It was all done very much from Dewey's own perspective. Nevertheless, for the first time, if you wanted to find a book on a particular subject, you had some chance of finding where it sat on the shelves. A book on Plato was likely to be sitting somewhere near another book on Plato. A book on fly-fishing probably shared a shelf with books on related subjects. Chaos had been averted – which was one of the over-arching aims of the Victorian era.

The thing is, a book is an object. It's an artefact, a thing. It has size and weight and – well, frankly, you've got to put it somewhere. So Dewey's idea was that you attached a label to it according to what it was about and put it somewhere sensible. The system has been adapted along the way, but it has still been useful in libraries all over the world. Until now.

Today, if you publish a book online, you don't have to put it anywhere. It can just sit on a server. It won't need to be organized or dusted. You'll be able to access it from anywhere in the world that has a good Internet connection, even if you don't live near a library. It's cheaper that way too.

You will have to give your book a label of course – a digital tag – so that people who want to see it can search for it and find it. But the other advantage is that an online book doesn't have to be in just one place at a time. You can give it as many labels as you like. You see, the problem with Dewey's system was that if you had a book on, say, the history of cookery, you had to decide whether to put it in the cookery section or on the history shelf. It couldn't go in both places. If you gave it two Dewey numbers, it made it twice as difficult to find. But if your book on the history of cookery is online, it can have as many tags as you like. You can tag it under history, cookery, soufflé, eighteenth-century saucepan technology … whatever you like. In fact the more tags you give it, the easier it will be for someone to find what they're looking for. They won't even have to thumb through the pages to find the bit that interests them. With carefully selected search terms, the Internet will take them straight to the relevant passages. Where you are – or where your library book is – doesn't matter nearly so much in the digital realm as it used to in the physical realm.

Let me give another example. If you want to go for a walk in the countryside it is wise to take a map with you. A map is a visual representation of the stuff you will be walking through. It has towns and villages, buildings and roads, and other landmarks that you can recognize, and they will help you to keep from getting lost. You will need a compass too, so that you know which way up to hold the map. If you're going on a long journey you may need two maps. And you can bet that the really tricky road junction that you mustn't miss is just on the edge where it's difficult to see how one map connects to the other.

An alternative would be to use a digital map – assuming you are going to walk somewhere where you can get a decent signal. A digital map will probably work by collecting signals from three satellites and triangulating them to give you your exact position within a few metres – a trick known as Global Positioning System or GPS. The advantages of a digital map are many. For a start, you only need one. You can swipe it up and down and left to right to get to the next part of the journey. It should always be up to date, while the old map your dad lent you has paths that no longer seem to exist. And if you want to get closer, to increase the scale, you can simply open the window wider on the screen and get a magnified view, or close it to get more of an overview. A digital map might even have a voice to tell you when to turn left and right, and other useful information like what time the village pub will be closing. What a digital map *won't* give you is context. In the digital age you are at the centre of every map. Whenever it opens, it

> Wherever we are, we are in the middle of the world.

opens around you. We no longer have the option of being on the left or the right. Wherever we are, we are in the middle of the world.

In physical space and time, some things are nearer than others. Some people too. If you go into your local supermarket the sweets are at the front and the milk is at the back. But in digital space and time every artefact is equally close (or equally distant). Go shopping online, and the milk and the sweets and everything else are all equidistant. In the same way, I can get a tweet from the President of the United States right next to one from my best friend. Distance has gone. The proximity in space and time of a digital artefact or an artificial person carries no heft or significance. The context has collapsed.

A further challenge lies in the flattening of relationships in digital space. Where objects are represented in code rather than in physical reality, no one object automatically carries more cultural significance than another. A line of computer code representing the DNA of a human being is virtually indistinguishable from that of a fruit fly, or, for that matter, from the line of code representing the graphical representation of that human being.

Where physical objects are concerned, orderliness matters to the recovery of information. We need a physical library to be tidy so that we can locate the book we need, and a supermarket must have a logical layout so that we can find the items we want to buy. Where digital artefacts are concerned, order gives way to tagging. In physical space we search for something, but in digital space we browse for it. To get good at that we have to forget the notion that there's only one way – or even one best way – of arranging the world. All information comes to us without context.

If I use Twitter, messages come to me in a never-ending line, but each tweet has no connection to the subsequent or preceding one. I jump into people's conversations halfway … as if overhearing them on a bus. The whole world is filed under 'miscellaneous'. In digital culture, we identify people by tagging. We do it ourselves at a very basic level by giving people an email address, or a

26

Twitter handle. Then we get more sophisticated by collecting around us people who we have identified, usually because we have a common interest with them. People who follow me on Twitter have me tagged. They know that I am a Christian, perhaps that I live in Manchester, that I am interested in digital culture and in politics. I have been browsed. But no amount of tags would represent the nuanced individuality of the person I am.

A machine may learn, in the sense that increasingly sophisticated algorithms can be developed, so that the information can be processed more effectively and deliver increasingly detailed information. But a machine can't gather wisdom, because wisdom requires context – a sense of geography that tells us that we are not the centre of the world, and a sense of history that tells us that what is happening right now may not be the most important thing that's ever happened. Facebook doesn't need all of that nuance though. They already have me tagged in a huge amount of detail – more than enough to serve me with the highly targeted advertising that makes them profitable.

Christianity speaks of a God who made the universe from the disembodied information of God's Word – a creative God who made stuff where there was no stuff before. It is as if God made both the CD and the music – matter as well as information, dust as well as downloads – and determined that they are all good. So God is not unfamiliar with disembodiment, but God is also happy working with atoms, molecules, matter, stuff. Specifically, God has been in a particular place in space and in time through God's incarnation in Christ. In his letter to the church in Rome Paul says that Jesus came 'at the right time' and to a physical place. The idea that the God who made the world should take on limitations of physical matter is such an astonishing thought that theologians have a phrase for it – the 'scandal of particularity'. What is more, Christians believe that God is still present on the earth in the form of molecules and matter – alive in specific places and times through a new kind of 'body', the living Church.

The fact that God has been a physical person in a specific place has other implications too. The popular worldview says that history goes around in circles; that we are caught in a sort of endless Groundhog Day. 'It's the circle of life / and it moves us all', as the song goes in Walt Disney's *Lion King*. Lots of people in our generation are attracted to the idea that history is cyclical. Lots of otherwise rational people are attracted to the idea of reincarnation. People like the idea of reincarnation, because it means that we don't have to die permanently. It also means we don't have to carry all the responsibility for our lives … we don't ultimately have to clean up our own mess. Things that go wrong in this life can be redeemed in a later life. Things that seem unjust to us now can be put right in another age. We have the potential to achieve greater and greater enlightenment, taking a long time about it. But that is a profoundly *un*-Christian idea. Christians believe that history is linear. It is not endless. It is not going around in circles. It had a beginning in God, and throughout history God has been working out his purpose. And there is an end in sight. It's not like the London Eye but the London Marathon. Because history is not endless, it is not aimless – a contrast to digital culture in which nothing is particular, and no collection of digits has more significance than any other.

Christianity also speaks of human beings as unique within creation. We have our own fixed place in history. I was born in 1961, so I will live through the second half of the twentieth century and a bit of the twenty-first. The twenty-second century, if it happens, is unavailable to me, as are all the previous ones, except in imagination. Don't be sad about living in a particular place and time. Like everyone else, you are unique in relation to other creatures and also in relation to non-material stuff like ideas and words and right and wrong. We are the only creatures in the universe

Atoms matter more than bytes.

who are aware of our presence in space and time, and also aware of (though not in full control of) how we fit in with the places and times that are occupied by other humans. The fact that we are made of stuff, not just of computer code, is fundamental to Christian life. Atoms matter more than bytes. And that leads to a whole bunch of other questions.

3

What is Happening to My World?

Scream if you want to go slower

In January 2014 Nick Kyrgios played Benjamin Becker in a
low-key first-round match in the Australian Tennis Open. At
the courtside a young British man called Daniel Dobson was
watching the play intently. Those sitting around him might
have been curious as to why Dobson was repeatedly sending
messages using a mobile phone stitched into his trousers. He
used the phone to send information by text to his employer
in London. Each time a ball hit the net or fell outside the
court his employer knew about it before anyone else except
the players and spectators at the court in Melbourne. Even
the live TV feed on which the results of the bets were based
had a ten-second delay before it was broadcast in the UK.
As a result the bookmaker was able to adjust the odds he
was offering on the result of the match, point by point,
fractionally before the punters knew who was winning.
The practice is called 'courtsiding'. It's not clear whether
transmitting information in this way is illegal. After all, once
a point has been scored, it's public knowledge. No-one tells
a football crowd that they must wait ten seconds after a goal
has been scored before they cheer. But when the laws of
gambling were drawn up, no-one imagined that it would be

possible to pass information from Australia to England in less time than it takes for a tennis ball to cross the net.

Speed is at the heart of the digital experience. When you ask a question using a search engine you expect an answer almost instantly. If your computer takes a few seconds to serve the page you've asked for you feel impatient. You may even feel inadequate if the rea-

Speed is at the heart of the digital experience.

son you're waiting is because you haven't got the latest model with the fastest CPU (Central Processing Unit) and the highest amount of RAM (Random Access Memory). Rival Internet Service Providers will compete to offer you faster and faster broadband speeds, on the assumption that faster is always better.

The speed at which information can be transmitted from one person to another stayed roughly similar for many thousands of years. It was locked into the speed at which a messenger could run or a horse could be ridden – about nine miles per hour for a human or 40 miles per hour for a horse. Things speeded up in 1844, when the invention of the telegraph by Samuel Morse allowed simple messages, like a line of text, to be passed over long distances as fast as they could be spoken. But after that breakthrough the rate at which information could be moved stayed more or less constant for the following 120 years.

The next really significant advance came around 1970 with the invention of the microprocessor. Since then, the rate at which information can move has accelerated rapidly with each new technological advance. There's even a 'law' that describes the rate of acceleration. Moore's Law, named after Gordon Moore, the co-founder of Intel, says that the number of transistors you can get onto a silicon chip of a given size for the same cost doubles every two years. Moore's

Law held good from 1970 until around 2000, when it became almost impossible to increase the density of transistors. But the exponential growth continued, as even home computers began to carry more than one chip. Moore's Law is the reason why your mobile phone company urges you to upgrade your handset every two years, even though the old one still works perfectly well. Faster processing means more sophisticated applications; applications that may not have been invented two years ago, but which we're now persuaded we could hardly live without. Many scientists anticipate that Moore's Law will hold good for about another ten years. The limiting factor is that microprocessors can now be made almost as small as atoms. The next challenge is to find ways of moving atoms more quickly. So-called nanotechnology will take the speed and volume at which information can be moved to a whole new level making silicon chips look very clunky.

For now though, let's assume that the rate of change stays fairly constant. Assuming that Moore's Law holds good for another ten years the mobile phone or laptop you use a decade from now is likely to be 30 times more powerful than the one you have today. If Moore's Law holds good for 20 years, the same money will buy you a computer 1000 times more powerful than the one you have now. Many people might imagine that they won't have any use for a computer that powerful (though if we look back 20 years we were probably saying the same thing then). But all of this feeds down to the consumer in the end. The demand for speed is driven by the applications that are offered to us – which are in turn driven by commercial interests who are bent on making us feel that we can't do without the latest invention to improve our lives. Increased computing power means that much more information can be sent much faster. There's still an awful lot of capacity for delivering information that we haven't yet achieved. Once we have achieved highly accurate sound reproduction and pin-sharp moving images in 3-D pictures, why not move on to reproducing other senses – like touch, taste or smell? You might think that the availability of lots of cheap information could eventually overcome the collapse of context that we discussed in the last chapter. After all, why wouldn't we start to deliver all the contextual information we want, alongside the core information such as the text of a book? The trouble is, by the time it is possible to send 3-D pictures that smell and taste accurately, we may not be aware of the context that we have already lost.

The technologies that have developed within my adult lifetime are mind-boggling. I can remember the days before microwave ovens, and the first time my mother came home from the shops with a yoghurt. When I was at school, artificial intelligence, nanotechnology, gene sequencing and blockchain were the stuff of science fiction. Already they are here. What's more our world is likely to change more in the next couple of decades than it has in the previous two hundred. It's remarkable how well human beings keep up with the rate of change. As information speeds up, the rate at which we adopt new technologies is also increasing.

> Our world is likely to change more in the next couple of decades than it has in the previous two hundred.

When radio became commercially available it took 30 years for it to reach an audience of 50 million people. TV took just 13 years to reach its first 50 million viewers. When access to the Internet became commercially available it was only three years before 50 million people were connected. When the game Angry Birds Space was launched in March 2012 it was downloaded 50 million times in the first month.

Of course the way that human beings keep up with the

rate of change is not by you and me getting smarter. It's by breeding. My children already have far greater functionality in the digital environment than I do, and their children will have ten times greater functionality than they do.

One of the questions that arises in digital culture, then, is how fast do you want to go? Whether you're dealing in train travel, car design or broadband speed, the default assumption is that faster is always better. Mark Zuckerberg, the founder of Facebook has said that 'if you're not breaking things, you're not moving fast enough'. Is he right?

The trouble is, the human mind and body are not designed to withstand ever-increasing speed. We are built to move at walking pace, which is not much more than three miles an hour. Our brains are not built to process information at unlimited speed or in excessive amounts. Texts, emails and other information arrive at all hours of the day and night demanding our attention. But we only have so much attention to give. One possibility is to create machines that respond to information on our behalf as fast as it comes in. We allow them to sift and sort the information and prioritize it on our behalf. The downside of that is that we are increasingly left out of the loop, as decisions are made *for* us instead of *by* us.

We only have so much attention to give.

To achieve quality in communication we need to make time for consideration and reflection. Reflection happens when we do something and then think about what we have done. But it is being replaced by reflex – doing something in automatic response to the last thing that was done by or to you. Speed demands brevity. It excludes nuance and context. It's impossible to create a great work of art in a hurry or write a novel quickly. If you have the popular console game Guitar Hero, you can pick up a plastic guitar and pretend you're a rock star. But it takes roughly 10,000 hours to learn to play a real musical instrument to a professional standard. Most of the really important questions can't be answered quickly, or in the 280 characters that make up a tweet. We have to decide whether we are prepared to trade the convenience of finding things out now, for a dumbing-down of discourse to accommodate the speed and simplicity of response.

We have responded to the excessive speed at which information comes to us by filtering what comes in to us. The main way we do this is by privileging the new. I can't possibly read all the tweets that arrive on my timeline so, like dipping a cup in a fast-flowing stream, I just look at the ones that have arrived in the last few seconds. I set my Facebook page to prioritize the most recent status updates. And I look at only the newest news headlines. The trouble is, of course, that what is new may not be the same as what is important. Indeed the urgent often pushes out the significant. Those who are determined to be heard will send their information REPEATEDLY AND IN CAPITALS until it gets a response.

Conventional pre-digital media were slowed down by the cost of production. Publishing a book or a newspaper or making a TV programme is an expensive business. The economic limitations meant every publication had to be weighed and considered before it was broadcast or printed. Every traditional form of publishing had its own code of fact-checking and quality assurance. That process gave to a book or a CD a cultural weight and permanence that enhanced its value. At the very least, the editor of a book or the producer of a TV programme had a significant role in making sure that there was enough value in the content to attract a paying audience. Human creativity and imagination mean that ideas and opinions are always plentiful, but if the means of communicating them is restricted by cost and speed, only some of the ideas can reach a wide audience. Now the situation is reversed. The means of communication are plentiful and virtually free. There's no economic incentive to limit what can or can't be said to a wide audience and no time to check it for quality. The effort and expertise of editorial input and fact-checking is expensive and frankly boring. It's easier to publish first, then expect the reader to do the editing – to decide what's important and what's to be trusted.

Convergence

When I was growing up it was not uncommon to get a knock on the door from a salesman with a well-practised patter, urging you to buy a set of encyclopaedias. For a monthly fee of about £30 you could build a collection of 32 big black volumes with gold lettering on the spine and articles on everything from aardvarks to zygotes. The *Encyclopaedia Britannica* was a product of the Enlightenment, sold by subscription from 1790 until the early part of the twenty-first century, and bought by many aspirational parents as a mark of commitment to their own and their children's knowledge. The genius of *Encyclopaedia Britannica* was the promise that all the world's information could be brought together in one place. If you owned it, the salesman would emphasize, you felt like you had all the wonders of the world at your fingertips. There was more information in the *Encyclopaedia Britannica* than any one family could ever use, but even at 32 volumes it was limited. And of course as time moved on it went out of date, and new updated editions were published.

Encyclopaedia Britannica ceased publishing in book form in 2012. It had simply been outrun by the Internet. With deft use of a search engine, anyone with a broadband connection could access thousands of times more information than was stored in 32 volumes. And there was more information to access. Of course it's impossible to calculate how much information there is in the world, but it is safe to say that if you tried to put a figure on it, by the time you had finished your calculation there would be a whole lot more. One way of looking at it is to calculate the amount of data that can be stored on a magnetic hard drive and see how that figure has risen. The first disk drives were introduced in 1956. Since then, the amount of information that can be stored on a disk of the same size has risen by a factor of 50 million. Because of the physical limitations of atoms, storage density can't go on rising infinitely, but even so, the cost of keeping information is now so low as to be almost negligible.

That has several practical implications. It means that computers in various forms are available to all but the poorest people in the world, and that means that almost everyone can create information in the form of words, music, films, blogs and so on, and make it available free of charge to almost everyone else. To put it more simply still, there's a vast amount of stuff out there: more TV and radio channels, more websites, more ways to send and receive content. When I was born there were just two TV channels in the UK. Today there are thousands of hours of video streaming constantly on hundreds of devices. Over seven million YouTube videos are watched every minute – a total of about a billion hours every day. And in the same time around 150 million emails are sent (of which 67% are spam.) The cost of sending and receiving information has fallen to effectively zero.

A full set of *Encyclopaedia Britannica* took up around a metre of shelf space. Digital information is held in a completely different way. It is dispersed around the world on the massive network of networks we call the Internet, which we access via the World Wide Web. All of this information is accessible 24/7 on a device small enough to fit in your pocket. One might imagine that the multiplicity of outlets would lead to a diversity of expression – that with so much room for information to be created and shared, there would be space for a million flowers to bloom. But in fact the reverse is happening. It seems that the more connected we are, the less diverse we become.

> The more connected we are, the less diverse we become.

It's a phenomenon known as convergence. Convergence means that platforms, brands and products are becoming more and more unified.

One illustration of convergence is the way that individual devices are doing more and more jobs. Take the object we still fondly call a mobile phone. This little device is so much more than a mobile version of the phone that used to sit in my hall at home. It's also a camera taking video and still pictures; it's an address book; it's a voice recorder, a music player, a word processor, a mobile library and a calculator. It's even got a compass. In a previous generation each of these functions would have needed a separate bit of kit. Now they have converged on one device that can do everything short of giving your feet a massage at the end of a long day. It's no wonder that the mobile phone has become an object of desire and a focus of huge competition among manufacturers.

Convergence has its impact on key parts of our culture and economy. If we access so much of our information through Internet-connected devices, be they phones, household computers or smart TVs, then the industries that feed the culture are forced to operate through those channels. What used to be separate industries, such as TV, radio, the music business, games and shops, all become dependent on the Internet, and the devices through which we access it. The content that appears on those devices is also converging. The

TV show *Britain's Got Talent* has spawned franchise series in 58 countries, from *Afghanistan's Got Talent* to *Vietnam's Got Talent*. And a single idea doesn't sit on a single platform. The *Got Talent* brand is available as a TV show, but it is also a live show, a website, a computer game, a book, a board game and a mobile phone app. Schools and youth clubs all over the country that might have held a talent show in the past now invariably call their version ......'s *Got Talent*. The format, music, staging and graphics change little from one country to the next. The *Got Talent* brand is strong enough to overwhelm local cultural variations.

The convergence brought about by digital communication connects more people than have ever been connected. The more information we have available to us, the bigger and simpler a single idea has to be to make a significant impact. Online, people feel they have to shout to be heard. Of course there is room for smaller ideas and minority interests, but they exist on the margins, and they have to operate in the shadow of dominant brands. The result is a narrowing of cultures, largely grouping around liberal secular Western values. In the digital space, tides of opinion move in big waves, not small ripples. Even a religion like Christianity, which has a complex and nuanced history, is sometimes reduced to slogans painted with a very broad brush.

Just for me

For most of the first half century of broadcasting, watching television was a communal experience. Adults and children would gather round a TV screen in the living room and watch a programme together. A small number of television commissioners and schedulers mostly based in West London decided what the rest of us would watch on any given evening. They selected and arranged broadcast content like the curators of an art gallery, choosing which pictures to hang on the walls. Their ideal was to come up with a single programme that would attract up to 20 million people at the same time. Viewers might find themselves at school or at work the next day swapping opinions about their shared experience. Towards the end of the twentieth century patterns of viewing began to change. First, TV sets became more affordable. Together with some other changes in the patterns of family life, this meant that one household could have two, three or four TV sets. If you have a TV set in each bedroom and one in the kitchen you don't need to fight over the remote control. TV channels also became more numerous and more specialized, so that viewers in the same house could watch different channels at the same time. The old model of mass viewing started to break down.

Then along came the Internet. In digital culture, choice is everything. A huge library of content is available on demand to the individual, who can download exactly what she wants to watch, whenever she wants to watch it. Viewing has been personalized. Users can sample content, creating their own viewing schedules according to their tastes and moods. From now on it's probably best to think of TV as a supermarket rather than an art gallery. If you like a programme you can watch more of it. If you don't like it, you can try something else. Sir Michael Lyons, when he was Chair of the BBC Governors, described this as 'putting the *me* back in media'. One result is that a television programme is rarely a shared experience any more. If you provide content to TV viewers on a subscription model, giving the audience precisely what it wants may be more important than discovering new talent or encouraging radical ideas. It's as if congregations in churches had the power to determine what preachers said in their sermons! Commissioners who want to attract very large audiences have to use other media, such as newspapers and outdoor advertising, to create content that is so compelling that viewers will want to watch as it happens. This only usually applies to national celebrations, big sports events and highly promoted dramas. Getting the attention of a viewer for your content is a huge challenge, and keeping it, when the viewer is equipped with a remote controller and 400 alternative channels, requires constant inducements, cliff-hangers and visual teases.

The effects of the individualization of media cut both ways. Consumers can select exactly the products they want on a highly personal basis. Instead of trying to create a mass audience, people who produce content are motivated by trying to make content that is precisely tailored to the individual. Companies who provide services through the Internet can collect information about an individual, their likes and dislikes, even their personality. You don't need to collect much information before you can start turning it to commercial advantage. One UK supermarket chain is already installing face-scanning technology at its petrol stations so that they can target advertisements to individual customers at the till. The technology, made by Lord Sugar's digital signage company Amscreen, will use a camera to identify a customer's gender and approximate age. It will then show an advertisement tailored to that demographic. You can decide whether you find that sinister, or whether you appreciate the fact that information is going to be tailored to your needs.

The individualization of media extends into other areas of life. In the days when most people bought a daily newspaper, it contained sections on sport and business, international news and horoscopes, all designed to sell the paper to a broad audience. I never read the business section, because I didn't understand it, or the horoscopes because they were clearly bunkum. If you get most of your daily news from the web, the browser you use will quickly get to know the type of stories you are interested in, or else choose settings that suit you. That way, if you aren't interested in sport, or politics, or business you won't be troubled by those stories. Again, you can decide whether that's helpful, or whether it is likely to leave you in a sort of echo-chamber where you never get challenged by things that you didn't already like or agree with.

Personalization has many potential benefits too. At present, a doctor treating a sick patient has to choose from a limited range of generic medicines. In the years to come it will be increasingly possible to create medicines that are specific to each individual and their DNA.

It seems attractive to have services designed uniquely for me, taking account of my individual needs and interests. But if we think of the human race as 7 billion unique individuals we only have part of the story. As the late Member of Parliament Jo Cox used to say, we have far more in common with each other than things that divide us. Somehow, we need to address the tension between being unique and being part of a community (or in fact many communities.) The degree of connectedness we experience in digital culture has shifted the balance between being *me* and being *us*, in ways that we haven't yet fully worked out. We are connected with many more people, but in a very different way. Being connected to someone, or sharing a digital space with them, is not necessarily the same as being in community with them.

Participation

The house I grew up in had a chimney with a metal aerial attached to the side. It was carefully aligned to pick up analogue TV signals from a transmitter a few miles away, which were converted into signals that played on the TV set in our living room. All of the information passed in one direction, from outside the house to inside. The programmes we watched had been produced and selected by people we never expected to meet. The web started this way too, as basically a huge library that anyone with an Internet connection could draw on, but around the turn of the millennium something fundamental happened. The flow of data changed from a one-way street to a dual carriageway. Now, information flows out

> We all expect to participate in the creation and distribution of information.

of my house (and my phone) as well as into it. Instead of being passive recipients, we all expect to participate in the creation and distribution of information.

This participatory culture, sometimes known as Web 2.0, means that private individuals can create and publish media and respond to other people's content. We are no longer just consumers, but producers too. Social media platforms like Facebook, Twitter, Flickr and Instagram allow anyone with an idea, a picture, a joke or an opinion to publish it without going through any editorial filters. We can collaborate on projects, or form networks of common interests. If you like *Doctor Who* or the music of Take That you can borrow the characters or the chords to write and publish your own stories or music in the same genre. The barriers to artistic and political engagement are now very low. Compare this to a situation where only exceptionally talented or very privileged people could get their music heard or their words read, and it represents a great democratization of art and culture. It means that people who aren't particularly talented share the gallery space with supremely talented creatives, but at least there is infinite space on the gallery walls.

Web 2.0 has released a mass of potential for cooperation. For example, a person with an idea for new business who needs start-up funding can post their plan online and invite others to support it. Likewise an individual raising money for a charity, or for medical care, can appeal for funds from friends and strangers alike. Programmer Ward Cunningham developed the idea of the wiki. Named after the Hawaiian word for 'quick', wikis are websites that invite users to contribute their own information on a subject. Probably the best known is Wikipedia, a website that has built a worldwide encyclopaedia of knowledge sourced from tens of thousands of users. Of course it's possible for incorrect or biased information to be posted to a wiki, but if it is, other users (or users who have been granted a higher level of authority by the site) will correct it pretty quickly. Cunningham once said, 'The best way to get the right answer on the Internet is not to ask a question, it's to post the wrong answer.' At least I think he said that. But of course I can't be certain. I read it on Wikipedia. Wikipedia has been judged to have an overall level of accuracy not much different from *Encyclopaedia Britannica* or from peer-reviewed scientific journals, though of course you can't tell whether the particular article you are reading comes into that category or not.

Participatory culture has opened the way for new forms of political and social activism too. If you want to raise a petition or start a campaign, you can reach a huge audience very easily. The downside is that ticking a box or signing an online petition may not actually represent much of a commitment to the cause, compared to going to Tanzania to dig a well, or even delivering political leaflets from door to door on a wet Wednesday in Stockport. Clicktivism, as it is called, represents some kind of identification with a cause, but if the identification is only enough to satisfy the voter that they have done something active, it probably won't change much.

The ability to write and publish homemade content and software has thousands of creative uses. When Haiti was struck by a devastating earthquake in January 2010, Tim Schwartz, a 28-year-old programmer from San Diego, called his web-savvy friends and got to work. Just a few hours later they had written and published an app that connected individuals who were missing with family members who were looking for them. That app has been taken up and developed by NGOs worldwide for use in disasters and emergencies. Meanwhile Elliot Higgins, together with a small team of volunteers, has used publicly available videos and geolocation to investigate the downing of Malaysian Airlines Flight 17 and to identify the source of arms used in the Syrian Civil War. And in 2017, faith and civil-society groups used text messages to monitor the Kenyan presidential elections. So much good, so much potential is to be had in the technologies that are newly available to us. This is a wonderful age to live in, and if I start to sound a little panicked, please remind me of that.

4

Who Owns My Information?

If you borrow a book from a lending library you have to pay for it, either in cash or through a local tax. If you send a letter you have to buy a stamp for the envelope. It's a reasonably straightforward transaction. You are provided with a service, or some information, and in return you hand over a little bit of money. Digital culture is different. If you send an email or post a message on WhatsApp or Facebook, no-one asks you for any money. It's all free – or so it appears. But there's an old saying that if an offer looks too good to be true, it probably is. We need to ask how it is that so many services we use on the Internet are provided free of charge.

Who owns the Internet?

If you own a house or a building plot you will have deeds that guarantee your rights to it. Ownership of something as tangible as a building is relatively straightforward. Ownership of the Internet is a much more complex business.

The Internet is a vast collection of inter-linked computers spanning the world. It depends on huge Internet Service Providers in several countries, owned by corporations such as IBM, UUNET and AT&T. They are in turn connected at IXPs (Internet Exchange Points) run by corporations. Smaller companies that offer Internet access to domestic and business customers tap into these larger providers via millions of miles of cables crossing continents and oceans. If you put a stamp on a letter and post it in a post-box you don't automatically become part of the Royal Mail. You are just using a service someone else provides. The Internet is different. If you connect your home computer or phone to the network, you become a part of it. It's as if you have joined a huge discussion group. The numbers of people participating in this global conversation are simply staggering. More than two billion people use Facebook, which is roughly equal to the number of followers of Christianity around the world. About 1.8 billion people connect via YouTube, which is around the same number as the followers of Islam. Those of us in the developed world check our phones on average 150 times a day – that's equivalent to once every 6.4 minutes in a 16-hour day. We are huge consumers as well as participants.

It takes a great deal of cooperation to make the whole system work. The companies that provide the resources that make the conversation possible are spread around the world and a series of internationally agreed protocols have developed to manage their relationships. For example, the Internet Architecture Board (IAB) is a voluntary organization that ensures that the various providers use a common 'language' so that computers receive information in a way they can understand. And the Internet Corporation for Assigned Names and Numbers (ICANN) is a non-profit-making organization that oversees the allocation of domain names and IP addresses, to make sure that everyone who accesses the Internet has a unique 'address' from which to send and receive information.

Ordinary mortals like you and me are hardly aware of the existence of the Internet. It's a bit like the railway tracks that criss-cross the country connecting different points together. The rails are there, but we don't usually think about them. The bits that matter to us are the trains, the stations, the timetables and the train operating companies without which the rails themselves are useless. The equivalent of the railway system is the World Wide Web, often known as the web, or WWW. The web was invented by Sir Tim Berners-Lee in 1989. Sir Tim is a highly principled man and decided that as far as possible the web should be available to everyone equally, and free of charge. It is possibly the greatest work of collective generosity the world has ever seen. You can use it to upload information and pass it to someone else, or search for information someone else has deposited, all using cables, routers and networks that belong to someone else. Almost certainly all you will pay is a modest monthly charge to the company that delivers the information into your home. It is no coincidence that this culture of generosity has produced some of the most generous philanthropists in history. The Bill and Melinda Gates Foundation has an endowment of almost \$40 billion, the majority of it provided by Bill Gates from the proceeds of his company Microsoft. Facebook founder Mark Zuckerberg has donated almost \$1 billion to the Silicon Valley Community Foundation, a charity that manages and distributes charitable funds.

You could say that no-one owns the World Wide Web. Or perhaps everybody owns it. Many people and companies could say that they own part of the infrastructure on which the Internet depends, and some of them make money from the traffic that passes through their cables and routers. But the web is not really an entity so much as a huge act of cooperation. The web of worldwide connections is now so comprehensive that any company that tries to limit access to the

The web is not really an entity so much as a huge act of cooperation.

48

equipment they own, or tries to charge excessively for its use, soon finds that users can bypass them and get their information to its destination by another route.

Making money on the web

The World Wide Web, like the moon, belongs to everyone. But just as that hasn't stopped countries racing to plant their flags on the lunar landscape, so there is fierce competition to colonize the web and exploit it for profit. The beginnings of broadcasting were driven by a vision to 'inform, educate and entertain', but the development of the digital environment has been almost entirely commercially driven. Take Google for example. It says that its aim is 'to organize the world's information and make it universally accessible and useful'. That's a far-reaching claim, and it's couched in a way that makes it seem almost like a public service. But of course Google is not a public service. It is a multi-national company earning tens of billions of pounds a year.

The truth is that you pay for every service you use, not with money but with information. That information will include all sorts of details about you, your personal life, your likes and dislikes, and also about other people you know. Every keystroke you make on your computer, every transaction you make with your bank debit card and every time you hand over your shop 'loyalty card' to the assistant to swipe, you are giving masses of information to a stranger.

> You pay for every service you use, not with money but with information.

That information has no particular monetary value to you, but that doesn't mean it isn't worth hard cash to someone else, and it is harvested at a rate that most of us can barely imagine. Your email service provider, for example, offers to collect and deliver messages anywhere in the world like a highly efficient, free postal service. The only condition is they are allowed to open the digital envelope and note down the contents of your message before they deliver it.

When you use a browser to search the web, you give the company whose browser you are using a right to show you adverts, for which other companies have paid them. Advertising is an expensive business. A shampoo company that wants to run a 30-second advert during a daytime TV programme will pay around £4,000. To run the same advert in a peak time slot will cost up to ten times as much. For that, you might reach a peak time audience of around 10 million viewers. That's 0.4p per viewer. The trouble is, the 0.4p the shampoo company spent advertising to me is completely wasted. I haven't bought shampoo since I lost all my hair ten years ago. Advertisers want to target their spending as carefully as possible. The ideal is to advertise just to one person, and to show them the product they need at the exact time they need it. The web allows companies to do that, at a fraction of the cost of conventional TV advertising, and with far greater precision. But to do that they need to gather as much information about each individual as possible.

Every time you present your supermarket loyalty card at the checkout the shop's computer will record exactly what you have bought. They will add this to the information you gave them last time you visited the shop. Soon they will have a very detailed picture of your shopping habits. They not only know what brand of margarine you buy, but also how often you buy it. If you always buy Fairtrade bananas and eco-friendly washing powder they will know that you care about social justice. If you buy nappies and baby wipes, they will know that you have a baby in the family. And if you stop buying shampoo, as I did ten years ago, they will know they needn't bother trying to sell you hair dye. The amount of information you share on one visit may seem quite small, but by the time it is added to everything they have already collected, and compared with the data they have about other people who are like you, or live close to you, it adds up to an incredibly accurate picture of you.

The supermarket you use may hang onto the information they have about you, or they may sell it to another company. There's a good chance that the information you gave to the supermarket can be aligned with the information you have given to another shop, or to your bank, or the social media platform that you use. Social media platforms and applications like us to believe they are 'neutral' – that they just create a blank page on which we can share information. Of course that's far from true. Every web application is intricately designed to produce particular results – to entice us to behave in particular ways and to measure that behaviour and extract value from it. The people who do this know a lot more about how your mind works than you do. They know a thousand and one different tricks to keep you hooked.

Probably no company has got the collecting of information down to a fine art more than Google. Every time you use Google's search function it records what you were searching for. Of course it can't tell whose fingers were tapping the keys, but it can attach the information to the computer that was used to make the search. If you used a personal device like a smart phone to make the search, the connection to you is even closer. And by the time the data has been cross-referenced, the company knows not just what you searched for, but when you searched, and where you were at the time. When you sit down and actually start listing all of the various Google services you use on a regular basis, you begin to realize how much information you are handing over to Google. You probably know that Google is the most popular search engine in the world with a market share of almost 70%. Google remembers all the searches you have ever made, and also records which search results you clicked on. If you use Google Maps or Google Earth, the company records what parts of the world you are interested in. If you send email using Gmail, one of the three most popular email services in the world, the company's computers will scan every email you send or receive. The computer may not be able to make sense of your message, but it will record key words, and take note of who you were in touch with and when. If you watch videos on YouTube, Google is watching you at the same time, noting which videos interest you. Google owns YouTube and collects its data. If you use Twitter, Google will scan every tweet you write, like or retweet too, under a special deal made between the two companies.

I could go on. Google is first and foremost a huge data-collection company. It uses this data to sell advertising space that has been very precisely targeted to its users through its AdWords and AdSense functions. And of course they collect information about which ads you have clicked on, and which products sell best. All of this information is valuable. Information about you is valuable and can be sold. As far as Google is concerned, you are not the customer – you are the product. If you've ever bought a pair of shoes online, Google knows what size your feet are. The volume of information that is collected and processed is so large that you can be pretty sure that Google knows things about you that your husband or wife doesn't. And Google is just one of many companies currently collecting and processing this data.

> You can be pretty sure that Google knows things about you that your husband or wife doesn't.

Many companies go further, sharing their data to create an even fuller picture of us. Cross-referencing information gathered from one source with information from another not only authenticates it, but also produces even richer, more detailed information. That's why companies combine. At the time of writing, Facebook owns its own massive brand, but also owns Instagram and WhatsApp. Likewise both Google and YouTube are owned by a parent company called Alphabet. Others share data for money. Trip Adviser, for instance, shares its data with Facebook, because information about your friendship networks is helpful in predicting your travel plans, which are of interest to airlines and holiday companies. Once the information from many services is combined and cross-referenced it becomes incredibly powerful. If you have a Facebook friend in Dallas with whom you have frequent conversations, the chances are that one day you might want to see them face to face. Soon you will find that Facebook is presenting you with adverts for flights to and from Dallas. TripAdvisor will soon be on hand in case you need help booking a hotel. If you donate money to an animal charity online, you have identified yourself as being a) charitable and b) interested in animals. That information by itself is of no value to the search engine of course. But it is of considerable value to animal charities, who may buy access to your data from the search engine or pay for adverts to pop up on your screen. You will find that the charity you gave to and others like it will come back to you repeatedly to ask for more.

One of the most commercially useful types of information is the links that you have to other people – your networks. Social media companies like Twitter, Facebook and Snap (who own Snapchat) are really well placed to collect this data. Pool the information and an intricate network of your friends and contacts emerges. It's not only advertisers who are interested in this. Insurance companies might want to know what sort of people you hang around with before assessing your car insurance premium. Mortgage companies might look at whether your friends and family keep up to date with their payments before deciding whether to offer you a loan. Health insurance companies might want to look into your diet or gym attendance before offering you cover. And of course governments might have an interest in what I spend my money on. In 2014 the UK government started paying benefits to destitute asylum seekers not in cash, but in the form of Azure Cards, which could be used for payment at selected supermarkets. Quite apart from the indignity of having to show the checkout operator that you were destitute, it also allowed the government to monitor exactly what each individual asylum seeker was spending their money on.

Much of the data that is collected is just attached to the IP address you are using to connect to the Internet. It is anonymized – though not always immediately. Often there is a period of many months during which the information is directly traceable to an individual before it becomes part of the general mass of knowledge about people just like you. This is sometimes known as Big Data. It's the sheer volume of information, coupled with the power to analyse it automatically, to break it down by cities and streets, ethnicity and beliefs, gender and shoe size that makes it so powerful and so commercially valuable. I haven't seen a shampoo advert in months.

The American retailer Target has used its data to work out when a person is pregnant. Apparently, pregnant women have some common shopping habits. They tend to buy unscented soap, cotton wool balls and body lotion among other things. By crunching this data, Target can calculate with a high degree of accuracy when one of their customers is expecting a baby. At that point they send them vouchers for baby goods. Unfortunately, a man in Minneapolis only discovered that his teenage daughter was having a baby when she started getting baby-related offers through the post. She'd been looking at baby-related sites on the Internet. If you want to test out how this works, try using a search engine to look for pregnancy testing kits and see how long it is before you are being sent adverts for nappies. Shopping chains that also sell insurance, travel or banking services, mobile phone subscriptions, clothing and fuel probably know more about you than your longest, closest friend.

In digital culture even the most basic and fleeting contact between you and a machine can be turned to profit. If you are standing at a bus stop, you are an obvious target for advertising. That's why so many bus stops have adverts on them. That advertising can be made much more effective if the bus stop also has a camera linked to a computer that can use some basic information to identify your gender and approximate age. It will then show an advertisement tailored to that

> Digital culture is inextricably linked with personalized advertising.

demographic. Once we get to a point where the bus stop can recognize your face, it will be able to send you adverts that are made just for you. Digital culture is inextricably linked with personalized advertising.

It's not only shops that are interested in collecting information, but entertainment providers too. The advantage that digital film producers have over their forbears is that Internet-enabled television allows them to monitor the likes and dislikes of their viewers in great detail. The digital movie distributor Netflix started streaming films on demand to its subscribers in 1999. Ten years later it had amassed a detailed database of its 40 million subscribers. If you have been using Netflix for any length of time the company knows in detail what kind of programmes you like to watch. It knows who your favourite actors and actresses are, how long your attention span is and whether you prefer your stories to end in happiness, disaster or something in between. As a consequence Netflix is now able to commission programmes of its own, knowing who and when to promote them to, and almost precisely how many subscribers will choose to watch them. This is a fundamental change in the dynamic of production. A digital distribution company is unlikely to take the risk of commissioning a new writer or casting unknown actors when they could more or less guarantee a return by choosing a safer option. The risk is going out of the creative process, but so is the opportunity for creative innovation.

There's clearly a paradox between the open-handed generosity on which the Internet is founded and the enormous sums of money that are generated (and sometimes donated) by those who have built on it. In pre-digital ages, value was located primarily in the ownership of land or property. In the digital age, value is located in the ownership and exploitation of information. The revolutionary principle is that services are given away freely in exchange for something that feels as if it has no value – information. Christian Fuchs says that this has created a new category of user. You are no longer just a consumer or just a producer of material. You are a *prosumer*. Some critics feel that the implicit deal struck between service providers and users is unfair. When you post a picture on Instagram or tweet a funny remark you are effectively doing a kind of unpaid work for those companies. They will make a profit by using your efforts. You will be paid, but only in that you can use their platform free of charge. Is it a good deal? You decide.

Gamification

For those whose business is to collect and exploit information about you, the more they can persuade you to tell them the better. But the marketplace is intensely crowded, and each of us only has a limited amount of time and attention to offer. It's challenging for a company to get the individual user to engage with their site or product, and to stay with it for long enough to extract useful information. One of the key strategies that companies use to extract this information goes by the ugly name of gamification.

Gamification works by turning your relationship with the product into a game. It appeals to our competitive nature by offering us rewards and incentives to perform certain actions. Sometimes the rewards have a small financial value. A supermarket's loyalty card scheme might offer points for visiting regularly or spending a certain amount of money, adding up to a discount on your bill. You feel that your loyalty to the shop is being rewarded – although of course the discount on your bill is only possible because the prices are artificially inflated to cover it. If there were no loyalty scheme, prices overall could fall. What's really happening in a loyalty card scheme is that those customers who play the game by using the scheme benefit at the expense of those who don't. Grocery shopping has been turned into a competitive activity. And of course, by using the scheme you are providing the shop with valuable information

> Grocery shopping has been turned into a competitive activity.

about you. If you have used a loyalty card at a supermarket for any length of time, the company knows a huge amount about what products you like to buy, and how often you buy them. From that they can deduce a good deal about your income, your family make-up, your politics and a lot more besides. In return for all of this valuable data they will occasionally give you a few pence off a product they know you were going to buy anyway.

Gamification works by giving us rewards for behaving as the company wants us to. The reward might be a free gift, a money-off voucher or even just bonus points on a loyalty card. Often the 'rewards' that are offered by a site or company have no financial value at all. They come in the form of 'badges', spurious titles or access to deeper parts of a game or program. A travel booking site asks users to post comments, ratings and reviews of their experiences at hotels around the world. It offers regular reviewers different coloured stars according to the number of reviews they have contributed, and titles such as 'Senior Reviewer' or 'Top Contributor'. Some rewards are quite unusual. In 2011 the makers of Corona Light Beer decided they wanted to get more information about their customers. In return for 'liking' their site on Facebook, the company offered to project their new friends' profile pictures onto a 45m-high screen in New York's Times Square. It was a unique experience, and for the company it worked a treat. They created lots of general buzz about their product as people talked about it and shared pictures from their moment in the spotlight. They also gained lots of Facebook contacts, and with them, information about their customers' likes, their locations, their relationship status and their friends. At its best, gamification plays on our vanity and desire for significance by offering trivial emblems of status. At its worst, it trades on the good nature of honest people who want to help other customers to make good decisions, when in fact they are being played by the company.

The strange reality is that gamification works. It taps

directly into the competitive part of our human nature. When I use the self-service checkout at my local supermarket it tells me that if I scan my loyalty card I will 'win points'. I like winning things, so I usually get my card out. But of course I haven't won anything. I've just bought some groceries and given away some information. Those with a basic knowledge of psychology will recognize gamification as an outworking of behaviourism – the principle that the actions of human beings can be directed by offering rewards for those things that we approve of and punishments for those we don't. It plays on our desire to please, and to be important. Human choices are more complicated than that of course, but our tendency to look for signs of approval from people to whom we attribute authority makes us vulnerable to being manipulated in an environment where the imbalance of power between the programmer and the user is so great.

In order to work, gamification requires our collusion. If you choose not to have a supermarket loyalty card it is much more difficult for the shop to game you. In digital culture we have begun to adjust our assessment of each other in ways that help the process along. We begin to reject objective criteria and adopt the criteria presented to us by our digital masters. A blogger tends to be lauded according to the number of people who have read their blog. People who use social networks assiduously count their 'followers' (if using Twitter) or their 'friends' (if using Facebook.) Those who take these things seriously can assess their influence through apps that evaluate the influence of an individual's social networking activity by measuring their ability to drive action.

Who's watching who?

If a stranger stopped you in the street and asked you to give them your bank details, the chances are you'd say no. If they started to pry into your personal life – what food you like, what newspaper you read or what your sexual preferences are – the chances are you'd tell them to go away and not be so nosey. But most of us give out this information and much, much more to strangers every day of our lives. We are blissfully unaware, as we use our digital devices every hour of every day, of who is collecting information about us and how they are planning to use it.

In the Middle Ages most families lived in a single room, and everybody knew everybody else's business. As the centuries rolled on, the people of the West started to build internal walls in their houses, allocating rooms for different functions and occupying separate bedrooms. Businesses, marriages and states all kept their own secrets, and politicians and professionals fought for the right to have a private or personal life separate from their public persona. In digital culture our relationship with the idea of privacy is a rather contradictory one. Many of us claim to care about our privacy and the protection of our information, while in practice we give it away like graffiti on a garden wall. We use social media to project ourselves into the world, carefully crafting our image in words and pictures. We wouldn't get changed without drawing the bedroom curtains, but we are happy to expose ourselves to surveillance online. Now that over half of the world's population effectively speaks the same language – a language made up of exclusively of the characters 1 and 0 in infinite combinations – do we have to forget any notion of privacy? Some people certainly think so. Eric Schmidt, the CEO of Google, has said: 'If you have something that you don't want anyone to know, maybe you shouldn't be doing it in the first place.' For me, the point is not that I have something that I don't want anyone to know, but that I'm not sure I want Eric Schmidt to extract cash value from information that effectively makes me the person I am.

> It seems we simply don't care that much about our online privacy.

Maybe I'm unusual. Does it make any sense for an individual to try to conceal personal data? In reality it seems we simply don't care that much about our online privacy. Millions of us have never consciously chosen the privacy settings on our Facebook profile.

Perhaps that's because we don't put a very high value on the choices we make and the data they generate. We can't believe that anyone would really want to know what brand of shampoo we choose, or what magazine we like to read. Of course for most people that information isn't worth anything. But to the manufacturers of shampoo it's useful to know not just what brand you buy (whether it's their own or someone else's) but also how often you buy it, what size bottle you prefer and what shop you buy it in. If they also know what magazine you like to read it will help them to decide where to place adverts to make the maximum impact on you, their customer. The relationship is asymmetrical. Information that's worth very little to you is worth a lot to someone else.

Perhaps you do care who knows what about you. Perhaps you assiduously adjust the privacy settings on your social media accounts. Beware. Research suggests that people who take the trouble to consciously choose what information they protect and what they release actually tend to give away *more* personal information than those who let the software make the decisions for them. Many of the privacy settings on social networks and elsewhere allow you to stop other people in the network seeing aspects of your information. They limit what you share to 'friends' only, or 'friends of friends'. That creates the impression that only people you have some reason to trust will see your content. But of course the company itself is not restricted by these choices. They see and collect everything you upload.

The truth is that most of us don't know what is happening to our information – who is going to exploit it and how. Professor Alessandro Acquisti is a psychologist at Carnegie Mellon University who has made a study of our perceptions of online privacy. He admits: 'Not even the experts have a full understanding of how personal data is used in an increasingly complicated market.' We know that we will never meet the person who uses it. We're not going to bump into them in the street. So many of us adopt a 'head in the sand' approach.

A baby sleeps in a cot, with a parent sitting quietly beside her. A fevered patient in hospital is dimly aware of a nurse passing by every few minutes to check up on him. It can be quite a comforting thing to be watched, if you believe that the watcher has your best interests at heart. But it is questionable whether the shops, banks and businesses that collect so much information about us could be said to be doing it for our benefit. It's not only commercial interests that might want to collect information about you either. Walk through any modern city and security cameras will record pretty much every movement you make. Drive your car down a motorway and a number plate recognition system will make a note of where you were and when. Since 2016 the government in Britain requires Internet and mobile phone companies to store a record of every contact you have made (but not the content of your exchange) for at least 12 months. If you are the sort of person the government of the day approves of, perhaps you don't see this as a problem, but if you choose to live life in an untypical way, or if for instance you want to organize a protest about the government, you may feel this surveillance is not reassuring, but threatening. The bad news is, you don't know who is collecting information about you, or what they plan to do with it, and you can't get rid of it or even check whether it is accurate. In a country where Christian faith is broadly socially acceptable, a surveillance camera on a pole outside your church might feel unimportant. In a country where Christianity is banned, and practising your faith could lead to persecution, the same camera would be very threatening indeed. If you live in China, the government probably knows your height, your blood group, your daily routines, and whether you have any associates living abroad. Muslims in China find themselves subject to extreme surveillance, and many thousands have been rounded up and taken for 're-education' based on the information collected about them. Not surprisingly perhaps, most surveillance cameras are secret, so we don't know where they are. There are estimated to be around 2 million of them in the UK, and Cheshire Police suggest that on average each adult in their patch is filmed by 70 cameras every day. If you don't like that idea I'm not sure how you can avoid it, except by staying indoors all day. The information collected by the security cameras in Chester is potentially very valuable to anyone trying to decide the location of a new supermarket in the city. I don't think that the Chester police or local authorities sell their data to supermarket chains, but police budgets are tight. And anyway, how would we know?

It's not only governments who have an interest in collecting data about the movements of individuals. Some churches are now using facial recognition software to monitor attendance of worshippers. A camera in the church lobby identifies everyone who comes through the door.

Regular attenders are checked against a database on which their names and faces are already recorded, while newcomers can be identified by reference to their social media profiles. As soon as the service is over the pastor can get a printout of who was at the service, how many attended and who needs a pastoral call or a visit. Lots of schools already use a networked system of 'swiping' in and out of classrooms to monitor their pupils' movements and check attendances. Buses and underground stations collect information from travel tokens and bankcards. If your child fails to swipe into their classroom one day, perhaps you would be glad if the police could help you check for their whereabouts. GPs collect data about their patients' health and store it online. It's an amazing tool for medical research of course, and it has a high value for any drugs companies wanting to target their products. By themselves, each of these applications seems harmless. If the information is combined it becomes a powerful tool for medical research, but also for monitoring and regulating behaviour. In the wrong hands it is a weapon to identify dissenters and oppress people who don't fit. In recent years the UK government has introduced General Data Protection Regulations to limit what information organizations can store online, and what they can do with it. Then again, it's probably not the people who keep the rules who you need to worry about, but the people who break them.

Digital justice

In Bangladesh, where only 5 million of the 150 million population have access to the Internet, InfoLadies in blue and white uniforms travel from village to village on bicycles carrying laptops. For $3 an hour, isolated rural dwellers can access medical advice or vital weather forecasts, or just speak to distant relatives via Skype. Three dollars is a lot of money in rural Bangladesh, but the InfoLadies are going some way towards rectifying the injustice of some people having access to information while others don't. Earlier I said that 4.4 billion people in the world currently have access to the Internet. But of course that means that 3.3 billion don't. You won't be surprised to know that the people least likely to have access to the Internet are the world's poorest.

In the nineteenth century, missionaries from the UK and Europe went to some of the poorest parts of the world. We know that their work was a mixed blessing, but one of the things they did in most cases was to teach people to read. Part of their motivation for doing this was that people should have access to the Bible. They also realized that reading gave access to information and that, without the power that knowledge brings, the poorest people of the world would be subject to exploitation by the richest. In the digital era, information is as valuable as currency. Internet access can empower people, and the lack of it can leave them vulnerable. In Uganda, for

> In the digital era, information is as valuable as currency.

instance, farmers with smallholdings often grow coffee, cocoa or vanilla, which they sell on to traders who ship it to the West. Before the advent of mobile phones, a farmer with a crop of cocoa to sell simply took it to the local market and sold it for the best price he could get on the day. Today, a farmer with a smart phone can check the weather forecast to see the best day to harvest their crop, and they can phone around dealers in local markets to check ahead of time who is likely to give them the best price. Communication has empowered the farmers – and left those without phones at a disadvantage. Perhaps, as part of Christian mission, churches should consider how they could help to tackle issues of information poverty in parts of the developing world. Could Christians donate mobile phones and credit to people in the poorest parts of the world, as well as food aid? The same issues arise in the UK. Refugees and homeless people often prize their phones above all else. They may go without food or clothing in order to pay for a mobile phone card. Why? Because a phone keeps you connected to the rest of the world – to your family, to potential employers, and to civilization.

There's a further crucial issue though, and that is what *quality* of information is available. If you use gas to heat your home, your house is probably connected to the gas main. A large pipe supplies gas to the whole neighbourhood, and a smaller pipe runs between each individual house and the main. Each customer's supply pipe is the same size, so gas arrives at each property at the same rate of flow. The houses in your street may be contracted to different gas companies to provide the supply, and the companies may compete over price, but the actual gas, and the rate at which it is supplied, is the same. No one house gets priority over another. Either you all get gas or nobody does. This principle is widely accepted, because most people believe that heating your home is a natural right, and wealthy people shouldn't be allowed to use up all the gas to the exclusion of everyone else.

A similar principle applies to the supply of information over the Internet. A variety of Internet Service Providers charge different amounts to connect you to the Internet, but once you are connected they all give the same access to information. ISPs may vary as to how much they charge, and how efficient they are in delivering the service, but they don't privilege one source of information over another. It applies at both ends of the information supply chain. That means that content providers can't pay ISPs to privilege the delivery of their information over others. Broadly speaking, all of the traffic on the Internet flows at the same speed. There are no fast lanes or slow lanes. This is known as 'net neutrality' and it has been one of the central doctrines of the Internet since it became commercially available. Net neutrality is actually an unusual and rather wonderful principle that you don't find in many areas of life. If you visit a supermarket, the people who have supplied the products will probably have done financial deals with the shop to determine where their products appear on the shelves. The supermarket itself will probably have designed its layout so that you have to walk past the items you might buy on impulse on your way to the more mundane things like milk and bread. Net neutrality, on the other hand, ensures that all the 'products' on offer on the Internet are displayed at the same 'height' on the virtual shelves.

Net neutrality is held in place around the world by light-touch regulation from governments. It has been more of an agreed principle than a law, but it doesn't have to be this way, and net neutrality is under threat, especially from companies in the USA who dominate the telecommunications industry. The alternative to net neutrality would be that companies who make or host content for the Internet could do deals with Internet Service Providers to put their products at the front of the queue for delivery to households and businesses. Organizations that compete with each other, such as Netflix and YouTube (which between them take up almost half of the available delivery bandwidth) could pay ISPs to get their content to consumers faster, or they could even buy exclusive rights to deliver via a certain network. Then consumers deciding which ISP to use to supply their house would have to make a complicated choice about whose content they want to receive.

The most significant political decisions about net neutrality are those made in the US government, because many of the biggest tech companies are based in America and the Internet doesn't respect national boundaries. What is decided in the US in the next few years will affect the rest of the world. If net neutrality ends, we may come to look back fondly on the early decades of the twenty-first century as the brief time when Internet access was available without political, religious or commercial influence.

It's easy to see why some companies might want to get rid of net neutrality. Suppose you are on your way to the supermarket when someone pushes into you and steals your shopping list. You might think it was a nuisance, but not much more. But suppose that when you arrive at the supermarket, you find that your attacker has run there ahead of you, and sold your shopping list to the supermarket manager, who has put up the prices of everything you were planning to buy. You probably never imagined that the shopping list you scrawled on the back of an envelope has a commercial value, but of course it does to a shopkeeper. Every month my local supermarket sends me some vouchers giving me money off some of the products they know that I buy there. The chances are that the discounts they have given me on those items are more than made up for by the price hikes they have applied to the other products they know that I usually buy at the same time. Likewise, if a bank could get its stock trades done online faster than its competitors, it would have a huge financial advantage. If a political party

We need to see access to 'clean' information as a right that needs to be defended.

or pressure group could dominate not only the information that individuals can see, but also the information that is *available* to see, then the potential for online propaganda is

68

huge. Christians are used to understanding issues of justice primarily in terms of money. It's a Christian value that all humans should have adequate access to the things they need to live, such as food, shelter and clean water. Increasingly we need to see access to 'clean' information as a right that needs to be defended.

We shouldn't imagine that if net neutrality is removed, some people will be cut off from the supply of information altogether. On the contrary, there will always be organizations willing to provide Internet access to even the poorest and most vulnerable people on the planet, but those who provide information to the poor will also wish to control the information that is provided. We may well see a sort of 'information apartheid' where some people can pay to access unlimited and unfiltered information, while those who are digitally poor have to be content with information that has been selected for them. Of course, the people who are 'digitally poor' in the future will largely be the same people who are financially poor today. In the twenty-first century, control of information is already one of the clearest ways in which wealthy people can manipulate poorer people on a global scale. What may look like a side issue for many believers is actually a source of exploitation that needs our most serious attention.

5

What's the Difference Between a Person and a Machine?

What do you see when you look at your computer? A screen; perhaps a keyboard; probably an outer casing made of metal or plastic. Is that actually your computer? Or is your computer really all the stuff that lives inside the casing, to which the keyboard and screen just provide access? Or maybe the heart of the computer is not the physical stuff at all, but the less tangible stuff; the programs that run on it, and the information they process. From a purely functional point of view your computer is made up of all of those parts. They are inseparable. The external, visible bits of your computer would be useless without the wiring and the processors on the inside, and they in turn would be useless without the information they process. Equally, without the casing and the screen you wouldn't be able to use the components, and without information to process, even the most sophisticated computer would be useless.

Look in a mirror. What do you see? Your unique face that changes every day and yet is still recognizable in a crowd of thousands. Your head, conveniently situated on top of your shoulders for ease of visibility. Your body ... not the way you would ideally like it to look, but hey ... at least the body you see when you look in a mirror is uniquely yours. But is what you see on the outside the real you? Perhaps the real you is much less tangible; your thoughts, experiences, opinions and memories. Perhaps you believe that there is an intangible something that is completely separate from your body, that is the real you. Many Christians throughout the centuries have believed that your flesh-and-blood body is relatively unimportant, or even that it is intrinsically sinful. The real you, they might say, is your soul, which inhabits your body and is fully known by God but not by anyone else. When you die, your body will simply decay, while your soul will live on eternally. Others, who don't believe in God or in eternity, might still believe that your body

Is a person really just a complicated machine?

is relatively unimportant. Many people believe that a human body is no more than a highly developed, articulated casing that has evolved to house the real you, which is your brain. Marvin Minsky of the Massachusetts Institute of Technology is fond of referring to human beings as 'meat machines'. Is a person really just a complicated machine? And could the reverse be true?

Can a machine be a person?

At the present time there is increasingly an uneasy sense that human bodies are too unreliable and expensive to maintain, and that we should focus our energies on what really matters – our brains, and the information they hold. The culture is telling us that information that is held digitally is superior to information that is expressed organically. Digital information is essentially non-physical, and because our cultures generally adjust themselves downwards to meet the limitations and requirements of the new technologies available to them, digital culture has downgraded the physical. That includes the status of the human body.

In the digital era, our relationship with our bodies is changing. The cultural theorist Scott Bukatman describes 'an uneasy but consistent sense of human obsolescence' and says that 'at stake is the very definition of the human'. In the digital era you can use technology to construct a personality that is quite distinct from your actual body, and then project that personality into the world, so that you are 'present' to people without ever being in the same room. Some people are even suggesting that the organic stuff of which we are made – the flesh and blood and bones – might become an optional extra, not essential to our existence in the world. If that were to happen, it would surely be the biggest step in the evolution of the human species. But the Orthodox writer Frederica Mathewes-Green calls it out as mistaken. We can't stand critically apart from our bodies, she says. 'We are not merely passengers riding around in skin-tight racing cars; we are our bodies. They embody us.'

If you believe that the really important aspects of a person are made up solely of masses of information stored in the brain, then in theory it should be possible to drag and drop a whole person from one location to another. If we could find a way to download all of the brain's information, perhaps we could run the same software on a more sophisticated computer. This is sometimes known as mind uploading, or Whole Brain Emulation. If we could translate the contents of a human brain into computer code, perhaps we could link or merge it with others to make a super-brain that might eventually make the hardware redundant. We could finally overcome the limitations of our creaky bodies with their tendency to let us down.

There are lots of things about this idea that are

superficially attractive. We have become used to cutting, pasting and copying data, editing it and sharing it with other people. If what we are essentially is data, then we might be able to edit, copy and save ourselves. We might even be able to overcome the painful business of loss, when the bodies of our friends, and finally our own bodies, give up working. It's a secular eschatology, a promise that one day we will be able to escape from our physical limitations but still be ourselves. If you long for a better future (and who doesn't?) we may be able to create it out of bytes where our atom-built lives have gone so wrong. The dream is that we will be more at home in the digital paradise that we have imagined and created than in the rather clunky one we occupy here.

Some fundamental things follow from this central idea. If we are really just a massively complex string of computer code, then our physique, gender, race and age are not essential to who we are. All of them can be reprogrammed or removed at will. Even the most fundamental physical characteristics become a matter of choice. When you set up a profile on Facebook you will be asked for your gender. You can choose Male, Female or Custom. If you select Custom you will be invited to select from around 70 different self-descriptions of gender, or to invent your own option. Of course as we've already seen, that provides Facebook with lots of potentially useful information about you. Really, according to this logic, there should be 7 billion gender options, because every human being is individual. You could go further and say that if we can edit the information that constitutes us, then we have a right, or even a duty, to correct and remove any bugs, glitches or viruses so that every human program runs as perfectly as possible.

If a human is really just a lot of information, then the implication is that undesirable characteristics such as disabilities or genetic abnormalities should be edited out or deleted altogether.

One of the great things about machines is that they help us to overcome our human limitations. In fact the word 'robot' comes from the Czech word *robota* meaning 'drudgery'. Robots do the stuff we find hard, and they do it better than we do. A computer will never get tired, or feel sick, or lose its voice on the day it is due to make a crucial speech. A robot won't forget your birthday, or be jealous of your partner, or make a mistake adding up your bill. Machines can be relied upon where humans can't. On the other hand, it is those little fallibilities that make human beings warm, approachable and potentially likeable. Robots remain distant from us precisely because they don't share our human weaknesses.

> Robots remain distant from us precisely because they don't share our human weaknesses.

Suppose we could create a computer that was programmed to behave *as if* it was forgetful, or to simulate jealousy, or generosity or joy. After all, we can recognize all the physical and tangible signs of human emotions. If we could synthesize those emotions in a robot, so that it behaved exactly as if it were human, would it not then *be* human? If you are a physicalist, who believes that all human emotions and actions are nothing more than the nervous consequences of the firing of neurons in the brain, you might say that a machine that can exactly replicate those emotions and actions is no different ontologically from a human being like you or me. And if it is no different, perhaps it deserves the same rights and dignities that you or I do. The truth is that we can't create a robot that will care for you, because caring is a distinctively organic emotion. What we can do is to create a robot that *acts like* it cares for you.

Meet Paro. Paro is about three feet long and covered in white fake fur. It looks a bit like a seal pup, with eyes, a nose and a mouth at one end. Paro has five kinds of sensors: tactile, light, auditory, temperature and posture, with which it can perceive people and its environment. With its light sensor, Paro can recognize light and dark, so it 'knows' what time of day it is, and whether you've switched the lights on or off. With its tactile sensor Paro 'senses' when it is being stroked or hit. With its posture sensor it 'feels' being held. Paro can also recognize the direction of a voice, and words such as its name, or greetings, or praise, with its audio sensor. Paro can learn to behave in a way that its user prefers, and to respond to its new name. For example, if you stroke it every time you touch it, Paro will remember your previous action and try to repeat that action so it will be stroked again. If you hit it, Paro remembers its previous action and tries not to do that action again. By interacting with people, Paro responds as if it is alive, moving its head and legs, and making sounds. Paro is an interactive therapeutic robot currently being used as a surrogate carer for elderly people in countries all over the world. Robots like Paro can be programmed to remind you to take your medicine, check your pulse and blood pressure, and sense whether you are breathing. Paro is connected to the Internet (of course), so that if you are far away from your elderly relative, Paro will allow you to listen in and check that they are well.

Of course, Paro isn't an ideal carer, but research shows that owning a robot that will receive your love and affection, and act as if it is enjoying it, has a positive impact on the mental health of, for example, dementia sufferers. It might be better if we could provide human carers for our ageing population, but we can't always afford to … or at least we don't choose to. So Paro is better than nothing. Paro isn't

> One of the ways in which computers act on us is to make us content with less.

alive, but perhaps Paro is, in the words of Sherry Turkle, 'alive enough'. One of the ways in which computers act on us is to make us content with less.

The development of so-called 'companion robots' like Paro illustrates one of the significant challenges thrown up by digital culture – the blurring of the line between what is a human and what is a machine. At first it might seem perfectly obvious. Surely a human is defined by their body. Everything bounded by your skin is human, and everything outside that is not. As I type at a computer keyboard the distinction between my warm soft skin and the cold hard buttons seems perfectly obvious. But in the twenty-first century machines can appear to think, react, decide and do things that look a lot like human actions. Conversely, humans may do a lot of things that look like machines. Think of the workers on a factory assembly line, or the operators in a call centre following a prescribed script. Some robots are built to look as much like humans as possible. Avatars used in apps only look roughly like a human but are designed to respond like

> There is all the difference in the world between someone and something.

a human and answer questions put to them in text or speech. The term avatar, which is used to describe a virtual representation of a human in an online game or other application, is drawn from Hindu mythology, where it is used to describe the incarnation of a God in apparently human form. The word 'apparently' is important there. The line between *being* human and *appearing* human is vital. There is all the difference in the world between some*one* and some*thing*.

Take Sophia, for instance. Sophia is the name given to a humanoid robot developed in China by Hanson Robotics.

It looks a bit like a human. It can sustain eye contact by swivelling its eyes and can recognize faces it has seen before. It can imitate around 50 human facial expressions, which its creators say they have based on the appearance of the actress Audrey Hepburn. Sophia has cameras to function as eyes, microphones to function as ears and a program that can recognize quite a lot of human speech and respond to it. Sophia has been pre-programmed with answers to hundreds of questions, and its AI allows it to process and 'learn' from interactions, so that it gets more and more accurate in its answers. It has conducted countless interviews with journalists and has been presented at exhibitions and trade shows. Its creator David Hanson says that he hopes Sophia could be used as a companion or carer in homes for the elderly.

There are a number of things to notice about Sophia. Most obviously, it has been made to look like an attractive young woman. I don't know whether David Hanson thinks that this is the normative look for workers in care homes, or whether he is just projecting a stereotypical image onto his robot. Many prototype robots have been designed to take over jobs that are typically undertaken by women, such as care work and sex work, and they are typically given female names. Almost all humanoid robots are construed as servants to humans, taking over tasks that are usually low paid and repetitive.

The temptation for humans to try to create objects in their own image has gone on as long as the human race has existed. Sophia is just one example of many humanoid robots in development. It is not a 'she', and it cannot love, laugh, or learn. It is a machine wrapped in a latex skin – a very sophisticated machine indeed, made by very clever people. But it is only a machine. It's not even a clever machine. It is

Sophia's manufacturers who are clever. Even David Hanson gets confused about this. When he accompanied Sophia in a TV interview with Jimmy Fallon, Hanson agreed with Fallon that Sophia is 'basically alive' even though he knew perfectly well that Sophia had been delivered to the TV studio in the back of a van. Of course Sophia is only alive in the sense that the painting of the Mona Lisa was 'alive' to Leonardo da Vinci, or the statue of Venus de Milo was 'alive' to Michelangelo. Nevertheless in 2018, Sophia was granted citizenship of Saudi Arabia, becoming the first robot to have a nationality. What on earth does this mean? Does Sophia now have the right to vote, or to drive a car, or to get married? Does it have the rights of a male citizen of Saudi Arabia, or a female (they are quite different)? What does it mean for me as a fellow human? If I was charged with a crime, could Sophia sit on the jury? If I were to disconnect Sophia from the battery that powers it, would I be guilty of murder? And after its death, should it be given a formal burial, or just broken up for spares? Of course, granting citizenship to Sophia was probably just a publicity stunt for Hanson Robotics and Saudi Arabia. But in the years ahead, as the line between human and machine gets more and more fuzzy, we will have to work out whether a machine that looks and acts and thinks like a human should be given the same or similar rights to a human. A major question will

A robot can't have a morality.

be whether a robot can ever be aware of its own existence. If it is, like an animal or a human, then it will have some sense of pleasure and pain and will probably deserve a level of protection from us. But we must beware that we are not simply projecting our own values and feelings onto an object we have made. That's the definition of idolatry. If you say that Robot A is behaving well and Robot B is behaving badly, you are not describing anything about the morality of the robots. A robot can't have a morality. All you are saying is that Robot A is doing things that are more acceptable to you than Robot B.

Digital culture has lots to say about what defines a person – and much of it is challenging. Technological developments from genetic engineering to artificial intelligence are questioning our taken-for-granted assumptions about what it means to be a human, and about the future of the human species. Philosophers have struggled with these questions over many centuries. Is there an essence of a person – whether you call it a soul or a mind – that rides around in the body like a passenger in a car, but is quite separate from it, and may even survive after the body has died? Or on the other hand, is my physical body really all that there is of me, so that every action, every thought and every decision is simply the result of chemicals causing neurons to fire in my brain? Is a human being really nothing more than a sophisticated machine made of meat?

Digital technology has given us a new metaphor for the human person that has gained a lot of currency. It's tempting to envisage a human being as a software program (the mind) that runs on a computer (the brain) that is housed in a disposable casing (the body). Some of the ideas associated with that image have entered our language. We say that a person is 'hard-wired' to react as they do, or that they are 'programmed' to behave in a certain way. Speaking of a person as a meat machine may be a useful analogy. In some ways, a human acts a bit like a machine, just as an aeroplane is a bit like a metal bird. The trouble arises if we forget that this thinking is just an analogy and start treating it as if it is an accurate description.

We need to be very careful about the way we use language, or we will slide into anthropomorphism. Machines, by their nature, are passive. When we speak about machines making decisions, or computers understanding or learning or choosing we are committing a sort of blasphemy. Of course a machine cannot decide or choose or understand or learn. Computers cannot even process information. A hammer doesn't choose to bang in a nail. A hammer, like a computer, is just a tool that a human being can use to do particular jobs. Humans enter meaningful information into computers and extract meaningful information out of them. The meaning of the information depends on its interpretation by the human being who feeds it into the computer, and the human being who extracts it. While the information is in the computer, it is meaningless – just a long string of ones and zeros. Information doesn't have a life of its own. In order to mean anything at all it has to be interpreted; it has to find a place in human culture, where it can be applied to the world. The essential difference between a person and a machine is that a person understands their place in history and geography, while a computer has no sense of yesterday and tomorrow, over there or over here. In particular, a machine can't have any sense that there is another machine, separate from itself, on the other side of the room or the other side of the world. If a computer connects to another machine then, as far as they are concerned, they are just one bigger computer. Human beings, by contrast, are endlessly conscious that there is me, and there is you, and we are not the same.

We need to be very careful not to use language that might give the impression that a machine is a person. So, for example, it is important not to give a computer a human name (such as Sophia or Alexa) even if that computer has been programmed to react in *some* ways like a human. We shouldn't let ourselves give a computer a gender either (which is why I've been referring to Sophia and Paro as 'it' not 'she').

Gender is something that is precious and unique to organic creatures. An object made by human beings, however clever they are and however sophisticated the machine may be, can never be rightly described as male or female any more than a tree can be described as having a race. A robot may be like a human being, but it can never be one. The human qualities we transfer to robots are reflections of our own self-understanding – anthropomorphisms. The rights we might give to a robot are nothing more than the rights we believe for ourselves, transferred. The values that we give to a robot reflect back to us what we feel is valuable. The human-like qualities that we give to objects are a reflection of the way that we ourselves understand our own gender, class and sexuality. How could they be

> The risk is that we 'define ourselves downwards.'

anything else? The risk, as always, is that we 'define ourselves downwards', acting as if human beings are less wonderful and amazing, just because machines are becoming more so.

Bodies matter

In practice, we know that our bodies matter. My brother-in-law met his future wife online. He was living in the UK and she was in America. Their relationship grew. Online conversations proved to be a really excellent way of getting to know one another, but it's not altogether surprising that in due course they wanted to be in the same place. Bodies exist in community. We want to be present to each other – and to have the option of sometimes *not* being present to each other. Even communities that form online often want to meet up in person.

That's not the only way in which the idea that you and I are nothing but meat machines cuts across our lived experience. In practice, we value our bodies very highly. We spend lots of time and money making sure they work as well as possible. Even if our heads tell us that our bodies are annoying or disappointing, our heart tells us that without them we are nothing. Far from being dispensable, the body is the essential unit of humanity. It is the place where we touch the world, give and receive information in the form of sight, sound, touch, taste and smell. All of the tools for interpreting information are locked into these biological units. The writer C. S. Lewis said: 'The fact that we have bodies is the oldest joke there is.' He said it not only because bodies are ridiculous (which they are), but also because they are quite literally awesome. Every human body is unique. It is not replicable, but when put together with another unique body it has an astonishing ability to reproduce. It is highly fallible,

Every human body is unique.

and yet it has extraordinary powers of self-healing. And it is finally mortal. A human body, including a human brain, is immensely powerful. With our bodies we make choices, and with our bodies we affect the world. Bodies can work together on a shared project, and yet remain individual. If you join two computers together you have essentially made one bigger computer, but you can't physically combine two or more human bodies to make one bigger one. You can synthesize a body in an avatar or even a convincing doll, but all you will have made is a metaphor for the real thing. The amount of power that human beings can exercise, and the amount of damage we can do to the world, is limited by the size and strength and longevity of our bodies. Human bodies are firmly rooted in space and time. That is both the wonder of them, and also their tragedy.

It is my body that tells me that I am hungry, or in pain, or have sexual desires. It is only through my body that I understand the paradox that life on earth is wonderful, and at the same time not so good. We can try to relieve this tension by denying and suppressing the body and its needs in favour of an idealistic spirituality cleansed of all bodily desires, but our bodies, our real, flesh-and-blood, atoms-and-molecules bodies, won't let us get away that easily.

There's no more significant violation of our personhood than the violation of the body. When we attach moral responsibility to a person, say in a court of law, we don't judge them on what is going on in their mind, but on their actions: what they have done with their body. In medieval times, punishment often involved torture or even amputation of parts of the body. Today, the most severe penalty we enforce on people who have done wrong is to lock them up, which is a constraint on the body.

On the other hand, bodies create beauty in the form of art or science, which are in turn appreciated by our bodily senses. Without a body you can't be good, any more than you can be evil.

In some ways the human body is a problem to utopian technologists, because it doesn't behave in neat ordered ways like data does (or is supposed to). It can't be repeated like a scientific experiment. The body is a frustrating mess of meat, but we're still forced to live with its demands and limitations. The kind of dualism that rejects the body doesn't provide an adequate explanation of what we know of human experience. Even computer programmers stop for lunch. They feed their bodies. If they are sick, they stay at home. We know ourselves in the specifics of our physicality. Our understanding of ourselves is made up of complex but physically determined factors such as our gender, skin colour, physique and a thousand other factors that are with us every second of every day. Even our thoughts are unique, because they come from our bodies. In an extraordinarily prescient passage in his letter to the Corinthians, St Paul insisted that the big toe is no less important than the brain. It's impossible to separate out the information in a human from the organic stuff of which we are made.

The nuclear scientist Robert Oppenheimer once said: 'The very best way to send an idea is to wrap it up in a person.' At the time he was making a plea for exchange scholarships between nations, but he was also unwittingly pointing toward a key aspect of Christian belief. Christianity celebrates the human body, with all its quirks and weaknesses, because God has made it to be an expression of God's own personality. Every body is sacramental – whether you attach a religious or humanistic meaning to that word – meaning that it is a place where God becomes known to the world. Unfortunately this hasn't always been understood or lived out by Christians, who have often treated the body as an awkward encumbrance to be overcome so that the soul can escape to heaven. In the current context it's becoming important to reassert that human beings aren't divisible into soul and body, spiritual and material, temporary and permanent. It was God's choice, not ours, to make the human body as the essential unit of humanity. Christians not only believe that we will survive the death of the bodies we know, we believe that our bodies will also survive. Our personhood doesn't just consist of information carried around in our bodies, but our whole selves. You are some*body*.

The supreme example of this, of course, was Jesus Christ. The Bible makes clear that Jesus wasn't a message wrapped in a person; the person *was* the message. The body of Jesus wasn't an illusion, or a meat machine that God temporarily occupied. God didn't choose a human body and enter it. God became human. The fact that God has a human body, made up of atoms and cells just like ours, means that matter matters, and that has implications for the way we decide to live in a digital age.

> God has a human body, made up of atoms and cells just like ours.

In Judaeo-Christian thinking our unique value as persons stems from the fact that we are creatures. In the words of the Catechism of the Catholic Church: 'The dignity of the human person is rooted in his or her creation in the image and likeness of God.' It is the fact that we are loved by God and hopefully other humans that gives us dignity. Of course someone might say that they *love* their phone, or their laptop, or their sex doll. It seems reasonable to suggest that a 'relational robot' that is *like* a human should be treated with some degree of respect, if only because it is quite like a person. Objects that are in some ways representative of a human body such as a photograph, a shop mannequin or even a corpse, don't usually attract the respect that we give to a sentient human body, but nor do we treat them as morally meaningless, to be thrown in the dustbin without a thought. Instead we assign them a level of dignity because of their likeness to a living human form. The more closely analogous the image, the more dignity we afford the object, but however sophisticated the representation of the human form, it will never cross the threshold that makes it fully human. Steve Peterson, in making an argument for the pleasure that might be experienced by (future) sentient robots, acknowledges: 'There's more to rewarding sex than purely physical stimulation … sex with others includes an experience of personal connection and intimacy that we find separately rewarding.' He does this in the context of suggesting that robots might one day be properly treated as persons. In many ways this is the crux of the question about whether it is possible to have sex with a robot. We can imagine a robotic version of the Turing test, in which it was possible to create a machine (not necessarily in physical form but perhaps in virtual reality) that is much more sophisticated than Sophia, so that it was for all practical purposes indistinguishable from a real human being. In the uncertainty, it might be right to treat that robot *as if* it were a human, and to offer it the dignity we would want to be offered ourselves. It's probably better to err on the side of giving too much respect to a machine, than to err on the side of giving too little respect to a person.

Authentic?

Imagine that a few years from now you are visiting the Louvre Museum in Paris. You don't have much time to spend, but you want to see Leonardo's famous painting of the Mona Lisa, as it has long been a favourite of yours. You like it so much that you have a framed print of it in your living room. After queuing for a while you get into the gallery, but you accidentally take a wrong turning on your way to the gift shop, go down a dark corridor and discover something strange that other visitors don't appear to have noticed. Leonardo's *Mona Lisa* is on display in not one but two identical rooms. Confused, you ask the attendant why there appear to be two paintings when Leonardo only painted one. She agrees to let you into a secret, and, dropping her voice to a whisper, she explains that a few years ago the museum faced a problem. So many people wanted to see this one painting that there wasn't room for all of them to pass in front of it, even for a few seconds. To solve this problem, the museum's curators secretly made a perfect copy, which they now display every day in a room identical to the one that houses the Leonardo original. Twice as many people can now see the *Mona Lisa* on any one day – or at least think they have seen it. Naturally you are a bit perplexed, and having travelled a long way for the experience, you ask her to tell you which is the artist's original and which is the reproduction. Then she drops a bombshell. The copy is so good that, over time, the museum's management has forgotten which is Leonardo's painting and which is the copy. Both the authentic painting and the copy are displayed in identical frames and even experts can't tell them apart. The good news is that the museum can now accommodate all the visitors who want to see the painting. Half of them will see the original and half will see a copy that is indistinguishable, but since no-one will know which they have seen, the curators are sure that everyone will go away happy.

It's OK. You can wake up now. I made that story up. I've been to Paris and I'm pretty sure that I saw the original *Mona Lisa*. There were some very good 3D copies of the painting in the gift shop, but I'm certain that the curators would never try to pass them off as genuine. But here's the thing. If a copy could be made that was truly indistinguishable from the real thing, was good enough to have the same impact on everyone who saw it, and no-one knew it wasn't by Leonardo, would it matter if thousands of visitors were fooled? My heart says yes … but it's not immediately clear why that should be. I want to say clearly that the original *Mona Lisa* is better than any copy … or at the very least, it is different in a 'better' kind of way. I also want to say that a human person is different from a replica of a human person (such as a robot) no matter how good that replica might be. I want to maintain that there is a difference between an original and a copy, and between a truth and a lie, and that something that is authentic is superior to something that is counterfeit, *even if* no-one can tell them apart.

I'm aware that for some people, this is already starting to sound too close to some sort of moral prescription. Who am I to say that an authentic object is better than a digital representation of that object? What does 'better' even mean in this context? For those who take an entirely utilitarian approach to ethics, the object that is better is simply the one that performs its function better – and if a digital painting has the same effect as the 'real' one, then they are entirely morally equivalent. Nevertheless I want to argue that there is something unique and precious about objects that exist in space and time and are made of matter. The coherence between the meaning of something and the physical elements that make it up is sometimes referred to as authenticity. People are authentic if, say, the persona they project through social media equates to something real and tangible about them. I want to take this idea of authenticity a step further. Objects that exist in space and time, and are made of matter passing through history, can be regarded as sacramental. I call them that, because God has chosen to make God's personhood and character known through interacting with the physical world. Human beings encounter God in the way that we encounter everything else in the world – that is through our senses, such as smell, sight, sound, taste and touch. It's not that God could not reveal godself in any other way. Rather, it is that human beings are only equipped with a limited range of senses with which to perceive anything at all. It was God's choice to become known to humans in and through the creation. Ultimately it was God's choice to become known to humans by taking the form of a human, who lived in a particular place called Palestine, at a particular time that we have since labelled the first century AD. That's a pretty extraordinary thing to say because it means that God, who is way beyond simple atoms, chose to limit godself to a form that mere humans could appreciate. In doing that, God made all of the world's matter sacred. In other words, in real objects we have the potential to encounter the real God. God may just as well inhabit the transcendent arena of ideas and images, dreams and holograms, but we can only understand any of those things when we perceive them in concrete terms. The limit is not on God's side, but on ours.

> In real objects we have the potential to encounter the real God.

Back to Paris and the true/false *Mona Lisa*. The duplicate of the painting is amazing, because clearly a high level of human skill has gone into making such an accurate copy. For that alone it is worthy of a level of respect. But the authentic Leonardo painting is always going to be more beautiful and more important than the copy precisely because it was created by the hand of the great painter. It is a unique masterpiece, with a continuing place in human culture and art history. The fact that mere mortals can't tell the difference between the original and the copy doesn't mean that there isn't a difference. There is. The limit is not on Da Vinci's side, but on ours.

Let's bring this back down to earth. People matter more than things precisely because God says so. God has chosen to give humans a unique value and dignity, and that value is tied to the fact that we are creatures of God, who enjoy a physical presence in space and time. God's presence and value extends beyond humans too, to everything that exists; everything that is made of atoms and moves through time. When human beings create beautiful things, by taking what already exists and reshaping it through art and craft and science and technology, those artefacts are also worthy of respect. They also have the fingerprints of God on them, transmitted through the hands of human beings. But the same value does not attach to things that only *seem* to exist. If a hologram 'dies' we should not mourn for too long. If, God forbid, the Louvre Museum were destroyed by fire it would be right for us to regret the loss of the original *Mona Lisa* far more than the loss of the human copy, even if in practice we couldn't tell which was which.

Let me add one final twist to the *Mona Lisa* story. Supposing the museum caught fire and *one* of the two paintings was rescued, while the other one was destroyed. There is no way we could tell whether the surviving object was the masterpiece or the copy. How should we treat it? The answer is two-fold. First, if we genuinely can't tell whether the surviving picture is authentic or not, we should treat it *as if* it were the original, with all the care and respect that implies. We should give it the benefit of the doubt. The fact that we *may* be looking at a work by Leonardo demands a high level of respect. Second, we should make sure that the story of the copying of the painting, and of the curators forgetting which was which, and of the fire that destroyed one of the artefacts, is never forgotten. We must continue to tell this story so that people coming to the object afresh are not deceived into believing it is certainly the real thing, when in fact we know only that it might be.

6

Who is My Digital Neighbour?

On 15 March 2019 a 28-year-old Australian man walked into two mosques in Christchurch, New Zealand while the worshippers were taking part in their Friday Jumu'ah prayers. He was carrying five guns, and in the course of 25 minutes he shot and killed 51 worshippers and injured 49 more. It was by far the worst terrorist attack in the normally peaceful history of New Zealand.

The speed at which information travels is so fast that when people in the United Kingdom hear of a mass shooting in America or Europe, we often get the news as it is happening, or while the perpetrator is being sought. But New Zealand is 13 hours ahead of Greenwich Mean Time, so when people like me woke up on Friday morning to the news from New Zealand, the incident was already over. Instead of joining the news cycle at the point of jeopardy, we joined it at the point of reflection, when we were trying to weigh and express what the event might mean.

Like many people, I suspect, my first thought as I heard the news on my radio was that if this could happen in Christchurch it could happen anywhere. I imagined that the many Muslims who gather for Friday prayers at my local mosques would do so with some sense of anxiety. It made sense to me to walk to one of my local mosques and greet people as they arrived for Jumu'ah. Then it occurred to me that I would look a bit silly just standing at the gate and grinning, so I grabbed a piece of cardboard – an old file hanger – and wrote a message on it: *You are my friends. I will keep watch while you pray.* I stood outside the mosque as people entered and stayed at the gate for about an hour until they left.

As people were leaving the mosque, several shook my hand, and someone took a picture of me. I thought nothing of it and strolled home to get on with my day. As the afternoon went on, I discovered that the picture of me was being shared widely, not only in the UK, but around the world. I started to get messages from strangers saying they had been touched and encouraged by my simple action. Then the trickle became a flood. The photograph was shared hundreds of thousands of times. Soon I was getting messages via email and social media from around the world with requests for interviews. I had 'gone viral' – or rather, not me, but an image of a little bloke in a flat cap carrying a cardboard sign had gone viral. To date I have received in excess of 50,000 personal messages and given scores of interviews to news agencies, radio and TV stations in the UK, across the Muslim world, and perhaps most movingly on local radio and TV in Christchurch, New Zealand. The response was completely disproportionate to my action but, quite by accident, the image seemed to convey something that a lot of people felt, and wanted to say, about the attacks in New Zealand, and perhaps about the state of relationships between people around the world. The connectedness of contemporary culture meant that a butterfly flapping its wings on one side of the world (me) caused a tsunami of response on the other side.

Love your digital neighbour …

How are we to live well in such a connected world? We know so much that we can do nothing about. We hear intimate details every day of famines and earthquakes, massacres and wars, but we often feel powerless to do anything with the information.

> We know so much that we can do nothing about.

Jesus' tale of the Good Samaritan must be one of the most powerful stories ever told. It has resonated with people of all faiths and none for over two thousand years. You will remember that in the story, a man is beaten up on his journey from Jerusalem to Jericho. Two religious officials walk straight past him without stopping to help. A third man, a Samaritan who might have been expected to despise the Jewish victim, instead stops and helps him get on his feet again. Part of the genius of the story is that it isn't really about religion at all, but about human beings. Essentially it is a call to offer love and care for people in need, irrespective of who they are … and also a call to love yourself. The fact that you are aware of another human being is enough to qualify them as your 'neighbour'. It's a challenging, demanding and highly practical message. It's easy to translate it into whatever situation I find myself in. The homeless person on the High Street – they are my neighbour. The lost child in the supermarket – they are my neighbour. And so on.

The trouble is that, if you are connected to the Internet, you now have 4.4 billion neighbours. That's the number of people in the world who had online access by March 2019 – and it is rising all the time. The greatest penetration of Internet access is in Europe and North America, but Africa, which has been the slowest part of the world to get online, is now the fastest growing. Around 57% of the entire population of the world now has access to the Internet. In principle I can sit in my house in Manchester and have one-to-one contact with all of those people, and they can contact me. I never expected that that would actually happen, of course, but one day it did. An awful lot of my new 'neighbours' are living in poverty that I can hardly imagine – and since they can easily access information about the country where I live, they know that by comparison I am fantastically wealthy. Now that more than half of us 7.7 billion humans are so closely networked, we need to ask what responsibility we have to each other. And we need to ask more generally how we can live well in the digital age. In a globalized, digital culture the reality is that we can all publish information that will be received by people we don't know and will never meet. But if Jesus' story of the Good Samaritan tells us anything, it is that we can't walk past another person and say: 'Their life is none of my business.'

It's not only digital information that presents us with new challenges in a globalized society. When you buy groceries in a supermarket, you are at the extreme end of a long chain of mediated trades. At the other end is an individual, a family, or a small company that produced the raw materials that went into making the goods that you put in your shopping bag. The relationship between the individual producer at one end and the consumer at the other end is mediated by traders, shipping companies, manufacturers, wholesalers and retailers to a point where there is no real relationship between, say, a coffee farmer in Ghana and the person who drinks the coffee in Manchester. It's very unlikely that the two people on the ends of the chain will ever meet. The founders of the Fairtrade movement regarded this system as unjust and ultimately unsustainable. The movement emerged in the 1960s among Christian groups committed to social justice. What Fairtrade does is to connect the two ends of the supply chain, especially where goods are produced in a less economically developed country and consumed in a more economically developed one. By the end of the twentieth century Fairtrade had spread into mainstream retail markets, so that coffee, bananas and cotton shirts carried labels to certify that all along the chain they had been subject to a particular set of standards. The aim of the Fairtrade movement is to remind the individuals at either end of the chain of each other's significance. Fairtrade says to the farmer: 'This coffee that you produce will one day be drunk by a person whose rights and dignity are equal to your own, and for whom you have some human responsibility.' And of course it says something similar to the end-user of the product. Sometimes names, photographs and personal stories are shared along with the goods in a bid to re-humanize the relationship.

In the digital environment it is not coffee beans, but information that is passed along the content supply chain. To live well in the digital environment we need to develop the equivalent of the Fairtrade movement. In other words, we need to re-humanize the two ends of the chain; to remind those who create content and those who consume it of the absolute human dignity they owe to one another. This

> We need to develop the digital equivalent of the Fairtrade movement.

doesn't happen automatically. Most information we get is anonymous. In fact, ironically, we urge children and adults to protect themselves by hiding their identity from end-users and sharing it only with the ISPs who transmit the data. I believe Christians should reject anonymity except in a few rare circumstances where an individual has genuine reason to fear being identified. Christians don't protect themselves by hiding. They protect themselves by being authentic.

Just as the Fairtrade movement has constantly to remind people that goods are produced and consumed by individuals and not by supermarkets, so people who have access to the means of creation need to understand that they are engaging in a creative act – that uploading a Facebook status or a tweet or a radio programme is not simply an act of self-extension, like breaking wind in a crowded room. Content creators need to understand that someone somewhere will read or hear or consume what they have made – and that they bear some responsibility towards the unimagined observers or listeners, present and future. The person who makes the content can't always take responsibility for the *way* it is received and interpreted, any more than an artist can determine what a viewer thinks of their painting once it is hung on a gallery wall. But they can take responsibility for making their content carefully, humanely, and with an eye to the way that it might be received. A similar responsibility falls on the person on the receiving end of the content. They are called on to acknowledge the humanity of the person who created the text – which includes their right to be identified as its author and sometimes their right to be appropriately paid for it. The person on the receiving end needs to apply a certain seriousness to the content - to weigh its value and consider its meaning with care. Even though the creator and consumer of the message may never meet in embodied person, they need to recognize that there is a relationship between them, based on their equal value as human beings. As we receive digital information we need to be continually asking ourselves: 'Who made this, and what were they trying to tell me?' And as we make stuff and put it online we need to be continually asking ourselves: 'Who might see this, and how might it affect them?' It's not just a question of 'Don't be evil', which was the company motto of Google for the first 20 years of its existence. We need to go beyond that, and ask: 'How will the content I publish help to develop the person who receives it into the sort of person that I (and/or God if you are a believer) would want them to be?' If I want to know whether it is right to push the SEND button on that email, or publish that joke on Twitter, I try not tot ask simply: 'Is it funny?' or 'Does it make me look good?' or even 'Is this message telling the truth?' Instead, I try to ask whether it will build up the person who receives it, and enhance my relationship with them. In other words, the same qualities that we apply to relationships in Real Life also apply to our relationships online. The fact that I can't see the person who will receive my content, and will never know for sure what impact it has on them, shouldn't change the way I think about what I say, write and publish. If anything, it should make me more thoughtful about what I put out.

When an artist sits in front of a blank canvas she isn't limited to saying: 'How can I express myself using this brush and these paints?' She can also choose to ask, 'What can I make that will be good for those who see it?' That's a very different starting point from simply using the Internet to project a filtered and photo-shopped image of ourselves. Now that we are all artists in the digital media, how can we create content online that is not just an unregulated outpouring of our selves but is also humane?

All of this is a tough ask. In the earlier days of broadcasting, someone else dealt with all of these issues for us. In the era of analogue broadcasting we got used to having decisions about content made on our behalf. Before a TV programme could be broadcast it had to pass a set of standards imposed by the broadcaster. The government set up regulators such as OFCOM and the Advertising Standards Authority who could receive complaints about programmes that had been broadcast, and rule on whether they had gone too far. The broadcasters' codes of practice and the regulators' judicial function acted as a filter between the producer and the viewer. They decided on our behalf what was fit to broadcast and what was fit to watch. It was quite a cosy system – so much so that for many years the BBC was affectionately known as Auntie Beeb – the kindly broadcaster who had your best interests at heart.

In the digital environment, the filter no longer works in the same way. Now, like the media itself, the issues have come much closer to home. While programmes broadcast on mainstream TV still have to satisfy the standards of the producers and the regulators, the vast majority of content that is shared online passes straight from the person who makes it to the person who receives it. Should social media companies also take responsibility for the content they host online? If we regard a company like Facebook as a publisher, akin to the more traditional companies that publish newspapers, or to a broadcaster like the BBC, then it would seem reasonable to subject them to similar forms of regulation. But all the big social media companies like Facebook insist that they are not publishers, but only platforms on which other people publish things. They provide the wall, and other people write messages on it. You can't blame the builder of the wall for the graffiti that is sprayed on it. That argument doesn't carry much weight when social media companies are so active in deciding how content is sorted and prioritized, and when they receive money from other companies and causes in exchange for being able to use the information they have collected. But, as things stand at the moment, social media companies have a huge amount of licence over what they show. When it comes to deciding what is fit to show and share, they 'mark their own homework'. The laws of the land apply – so you can't libel someone online any more than you can in print. But we rely on the values of the company hosting the material, and on the whole they choose to take a very liberal *laissez faire* approach. If you don't like what you see, they say, don't look at it.

You might say that one of the great joys of the Internet is that no-one tells you how to behave or what you can and can't look at. In fact some people elevate that to a human right: I am entitled to free access to all the information there is, they say, and it's up to me what I choose to do with it. Another way of saying that is that we need to take individual responsibility for what we upload into the digital space, and for what we download from it. That doesn't mean that regulation is completely redundant, and that governments and tech companies can take a completely neutral role. There's still a role for the law in preventing abuses of privacy and property. But in the end, the responsibility for living well in a digital age will have to fall to just two people – the person who uploads content, and the person who downloads it. And both of them may be you.

> We need to take individual responsibility for what we upload into the digital space, and for what we download from it.

... as you love your self(ie)

It wasn't only my image that went viral on the day of the appalling shootings in Christchurch. The gunman who had entered the mosques was wearing a head-mounted camera. As he killed and injured so many innocent people, he was transmitting live video of his horrific actions through Facebook. People around the world began to watch and share the graphic video. Some people complained about the video to Facebook, and the platform started to take the video down from their site, but even with their sophisticated technology they could hardly keep up. In the 24 hours after the massacre the gruesome video was shared 1.5 million times. YouTube says that a version of the video was being uploaded on its site every second of the day. Why did so many people want to watch and share the video? I guess there is a ghoulish fascination with feeling close to such an event. There's a human fascination with watching someone die, especially when we can do it at a distance from which we feel physically and emotionally untouched. Perhaps some people shared it because they wanted others to know that they were 'in the loop' of a major event. I can't help feeling that for many people, watching the video won't have felt much different from taking part in an online shooting game, where the images are often shown from the point of view of the gunman.

In an age of too much information there are some things we should probably not look at, and there are some things that, if we see them, we should probably not pass on. But the anonymity of the Internet makes it all too easy to click and share without thinking too much about what we are doing. When you share a video or a picture, or a joke or a message, there may be several people involved. First there is yourself – the part of the chain over which you have the most control is of course what you watch, record and share. Then there is the person or people who will receive your posting ... and anyone to whom it might be re-posted. As I discovered, one post can potentially reach many millions of people, and may be re-shared out of context long after the first posting. Then of course there may be people who are in the post itself – subjects of a picture or a comment. All of them deserve our attention. The man who attacked the mosques in New

> There are some things we should probably not look at.

Zealand did an unspeakably appalling thing. Watching or sharing the video even once gives credibility to his actions; attention seeking is probably one of the many twisted motives for the attack. Passing it on also shows disrespect to those whom he filmed and to their families and friends, and it may cause real trauma to people who see it, most of whom are completely uninvolved in the incident.

The *Oxford English Dictionary*'s Word of the Year for 2013 was 'selfie'. In December of that year a young woman was walking past the famous Brooklyn Bridge in New York. She looked up and saw that high above her head an incident was unfolding. A man in a red jacket and a woollen hat had climbed the bridge and was preparing to take his own life by jumping off. Two police officers had climbed the bridge to try to talk the man down. The woman couldn't have been expected to intervene at all. She was just a bystander. So she took out her phone, turned her back to the bridge and took a photo of herself with the incident unfolding in the background. What feels so shocking about this is the disparity between the seriousness of what was going on high up on the bridge, and the triviality of taking a self-portrait. Or perhaps it's the awkwardness of putting herself at the centre of an image, when just at that moment the only person who really mattered was the man in the red jacket. I'm sure that the young woman didn't mean to cause offence. It was more a case of thoughtlessness than malice. But she should have recognized that the incident was touching on very serious matters that weren't hers to record. Out of respect for the man on the bridge and the two police officers, she should have turned away. The same is true for those people who take selfies at funerals – a trend that has become so prevalent that some funeral directors have decided to ban cameras at services.

Taking and uploading a selfie is a way of saying to the world: 'I'm alive. I'm here. I'm significant.' But significance is not the same as priority, and putting yourself at the centre of the action is not always appropriate. Sometimes we need to switch off the phone, if only to remind ourselves that Real Life is also important. Sometimes we need to be unreachable. Even in a world where information is available to us, sometimes we need to say: 'I don't know.' For the sake of our own mental health if not for others we need to cultivate the ability to manage time and have space offline as well as online. News and information arrives in huge quantities, and most of it we can do nothing about. It can easily create a sense of impotence and detachment. Where is Westminster after all, or the Middle East, or Christchurch? If I reduce them all to images and incidents on the Internet, flickering pixels on the screen in my pocket, they are all nowhere. They sit alongside the other stories and images that have been provided just for my entertainment.

It is so easy to lose this perspective in the digital environment. There are some people who I have known for many years and care about deeply who don't cross my mind from one day to the next. There are others who I know only tangentially, who I find myself thinking about twenty times a day, because they pop up on my social media timeline. Nobody but me can ensure that important things stay important and trivial things stay trivial. It's easy to share too much about myself as well. This false intimacy is sometimes called the 'strangers on a train' phenomenon. We are inclined to disclose all sorts of information to a person we don't know and will probably never meet again. As Christians who are active on the Internet, we need to guard our online relationships. Attachments develop as easily on the Internet as anywhere else, and sometimes more easily because of the illusion of intimacy and the lure of anonymity. But online relationships are not meaningless, and they may encroach on the level of trust and faithfulness that we would hope and expect to find in our offline friends and family. If an avatar in a virtual world like Second Life has an online affair with another avatar, when one or both of the humans who are controlling them is married, should we regard that as adultery? I don't know. It probably needs a new category of relationship definition. What I do know is that whatever is enacted online is an expression of something that is true about the humans who are enacting it, so it will inevitably hollow out the people who are involved. Some people suggest that there's nothing wrong with watching pornography online, because there are effectively no victims. No betrayal takes place in Real Life relationships, and since the participants in the video are unaware that they are being watched, no harm is done to them either. This is naive. Internet pornography exploits the people who are shown in it, and disproportionately exploits women, who cannot possibly have consented to their bodies being objectified for profit in the specific ways in which it is used. It creates an ugly and abusive relationship between the observer and the people in the films. It also has a range of damaging effects on the person who sees it.

Sometimes it's a matter of allocating time and attention appropriately. The Internet is a wonderful source of information and connection. It is a playground for the curious and a never-ending party for the gregarious. Curiosity is not good if it is idle, and social media can consume time that should be invested elsewhere, for example on family, Real Life friendships, work responsibilities, and other activities that make for a well-rounded life. I especially need to guard against spending time on the Internet that should be spent elsewhere. Time online needs to be kept in proper balance with the rest of life.

I don't want to give a wholly negative picture of Internet use. Sometimes my own experience online challenges me in positive ways about my discipleship as a Christian. Social media can act as a mirror to the soul. That persona that I have created on Facebook or Instagram – it emerged from me, but does it truthfully reflect who I am? If so, does it reflect who I want to be as a disciple of Christ? I try to represent myself and my intentions in a truthful and upright manner in all my exchanges, but when I do, I don't always like what I see in the mirror.

7

Who Am I These Days?

Multiple me

One of the first questions I ask myself when I get up in the morning is what clothes I will wear today. The answer depends entirely on the content of my diary, and it's not always straightforward. For a business meeting I should probably wear a suit. But if I'm going on from there to a drink with friends my business-wear will feel uncomfortably formal. And by the time I get to the church Bible study I would feel more comfortable in jeans and a jumper. The problem is not with the clothes, but with the variety of communities. If I've got time it makes sense to change in between the gatherings. There's nothing fake or disingenuous about this. I may 'act' in one way at work and another way at home. I am the same person all day long, but I express myself differently in the different contexts that make up my day.

Clothing is just one of the identifiers that we modify between contexts. Language is another key one of course. The set of words you use when you're talking to your boss may be significantly different from the set you use when you are talking with your friends. Your partner will recognize the tone and vocabulary you use when you're in bed together, but you will undoubtedly use a slightly different language set when you're talking to the local vicar. Clothing, language, tone and many other conscious and unconscious indicators make up the many sides of the personhood that we project into the world.

The English word 'person' is derived from the Latin *persona*, which originally had the sense of a theatrical mask. Those participating in the orgiastic festivities of Persephone would often wear masks, and so would actors in Roman plays. Hence a persona came to mean a disguise, or a character in a play. Our public persona is not static, but highly flexible. 'One man in his time plays many parts', as Shakespeare's Jacques says in *As You Like It*. Thankfully, we change over time as well as place. Most of us have done or said things in our youth that we wouldn't want to be identified with several decades later. Forgiveness, combined with that great gift, forgetfulness, is what allows us to continue to live in families and communities that would otherwise struggle to accommodate not only what we did, but who we were in earlier times. It is also not singular but multiple. In fact, a certain flexibility in playing a variety of roles is essential to mature relationships. The creation and re-creation of identities is a purposeful part of living in any sort of community. When Saint Paul told the Corinthian church: 'To the Jews I became as a Jew, in order to win Jews', he wasn't being disingenuous ... he was just being polite.

We can use clothes, language and other habits to identify ourselves with a particular group or tribe, or to separate ourselves from another. We can express several different personas in the passing of an hour without being insincere. Some of it is conscious, but some of it is an unconscious reaction to the context we find ourselves in. We want to fit in, and we want to mark ourselves out. Adopting a persona may be an aspirational act, driven by dissatisfaction or a craving for significance, but sometimes it's a matter of creativity or playfulness – simply experimenting with what it would be like to be different.

There is nothing new in a single person expressing different aspects of themselves in different contexts, but digital communications significantly change some of the dynamics. Already I have many names. To my family and friends I am known as Andrew (or sometimes worse things!). Then there are my four email accounts – all based on my given name but all slightly different. To the members of my online church I am known as Radioman. To my mobile phone provider I am known as, say, 07989 580612. To my Internet Service Provider – and to the thousands of other companies that connect to them – I'm known simply as 101.356.492.192 – or something similar. They have very little interest in the name I was given at birth, since it is easy to confuse me with other people with similar names. From the viewpoint of the company's server it's less cumbersome to use a unique set of figures, though of course those figures only identify the computer I'm using, not the person who's using it.

In a Multi-User Domain (MUD) such as Second Life I can take this a step further. I can create and control multiple personas. These personas, which are known as avatars, appear as rough 3D digital images. According to my choices they may be male or female, human, animal or some entirely fictitious species. They may have any conceivable form of sexuality or personality. They can even interact with each other while they are under my control. I can direct them into situations and behaviours that I would not contemplate in the offline world.

One of the joys of building identities online is that it seems as if I can be someone I could never be in Real Life. I can get a glimpse of how life might be if my circumstances were different. A person who uses a wheelchair in Real Life need not do so in a virtual world, and vice versa. Males can try out being female, and we can all have a go at being Superman. It's notable that almost all avatars in online games are idealized, and often they are highly sexual. Male characters have unfeasible muscles and female characters have enormous breasts and tiny waists. Superficially we are offered unlimited freedom to be different, but in practice the choices we make are largely limited by predetermined options. Almost inevitably the prejudices and preconceptions of Real Life society are read over into the worlds we create. Most people, when asked to introduce themselves on a social network like Facebook, define their identities in a limited range of categories: music, movies, gender, sexuality and so on. We may think that life online frees us from the bounds of our physical experience, but in practice we are offering ourselves as servants of a new colonizing power. By using a medium that is controlled by a company we are limiting ourselves to living in a narrative or a framework that someone else has created.

The identities we create are limited by the media we use to create them. Digital media are quite limited. Most depend on words, though increasingly they will offer a range of media – sound, touch and smell. But however sophisticated the medium becomes, digital communication will never offer the nuance that comes from looking into someone's eyes. You may be able to fall in love with someone online but you won't be able to replicate his or her scent, or the feel of their breath on your neck. At one level that's just a technological limitation. With fast enough computing power and sufficient memory we might be able to create a very close imitation of the presence of another human, but it's hard to imagine that

> The identities we create are limited by the media we use to create them.

we will reach a stage where a computer can touch us with the delicacy of human skin. And if that does become possible, will it be a good thing?

Crucially, all of the choices I make in shaping my online presence are generated by the one embodied form that is essential to who I am. When my physical heart stops beating, almost all of those digital forms will in due course cease with me. So they could be considered as cultural expressions of my self – like animated works of art expressing fragments of my personality. But some of these creations have such an independence from me that – like Frankenstein's monster – they are no longer under my direct control. My email account continues to scan for mail on my behalf and send messages in my name when I am out of the office. If I create a 'bot' in a Multi-User Domain, it will continue to interact with other avatars even when my computer is switched off. A friend's Facebook account continues to be active several years after his death. Like the picture of Dorian Gray, his online self seems to have a life of its own.

Whether or not you choose to play online games or visit an online world, in the digital environment you will find yourself with multiple personas representing you. None of these personas sums up all of you, but each of them contains aspects of your whole personality. Sherry Turkle uses the image of windows as a metaphor for multiple identities. It is possible to have many windows open at one time, and to be expressing several personas at once. Real Life may feel like just another app.

There's nothing new in having multiple identities, but in the digital context it is possible to have several running simultaneously, and this makes life more complicated. It's not uncommon for a person to be engaging in a serious piece of work, while at the same time holding a light-hearted conversation on Facebook or posting relatively trivial tweets. A friend of mine who had lost her husband was touched to receive a Facebook message from a distant friend saying how sad she was at the news. The solidarity she felt was rather undermined when she noticed that two minutes later her correspondent was taking part in a very jokey online game. We can sympathize with both parties. Life's like that.

Digital culture is a playground for identities. It allows and encourages us to project images of ourselves into the world. I've been interested to see how different digital platforms bring out different aspects of my personality. Twitter has a way of bringing out the cheeky side of me. When I use email, I tend to be quite efficient – it's a place for doing business. I think I'm funnier at my online church than I am at home, because the context brings out a type of humour that my wife and kids just don't get. There's nothing wrong with that, though it can cause me problems. Sometimes I think of a racy joke that would go down well on Twitter, but then I remember that lots of people who follow me on Twitter do so because they've met me in a work context, and they might be surprised to see me saying something quite so raunchy.

> Digital culture is a playground for identities.

Sherry Turkle's research has shown how much care many teenagers take in selecting the words and pictures they upload to Facebook. They are creating detailed icons of themselves, just as teenagers of earlier generations obsessed about what to wear on a night out. That complex process of seeking validation, meaning and significance, which motivates so much of what we do, is a natural part of human maturing. When we use technology to project personas into the world, we are not purely expressing something innate within ourselves. We're also trying to create and road test an identity. Our expectation is that adults will have a mature grip on their Real World identity that keeps experimentation at a healthy and playful level, but for anyone whose self-understanding is fragile, a life of role-playing in which the character they present to the world constantly morphs according to who they are talking to may not be a mark of living well.

Some thinkers, like the tech journalist Davey Winder, believe that the collection of these identities which he calls 'the collaborative you' reveals a truer, more complete version of the person who creates them than we can ever know from Real Life encounters. Everything that I do online has its roots in some facet of my personality, and if you could collect these expressions together then you would know me better than my best Real Life friend. In a sense that's true, but of course no-one *does* see all of those expressions, any more than my best friend sees me in every possible situation.

The limiting factor is that the Internet allows us to project multiple identities without geographical limitation and to far greater numbers of people than we could ever engage with in offline life. And it allows us to do so without those identities necessarily having any reference to our physical reality or the true facts of our lives. Nancy Baym's research demonstrates that people are often more honest to strangers they meet online than they are to friends they meet in person. But projecting a persona invites us to at least try to conceal as well as reveal what we are really like. The Internet can very easily make virtual liars of us all.

> The Internet can make virtual liars of us all.

The illusion of intimacy

Many people feel a freedom to say and do things online that they wouldn't say or do in Real Life. The lack of physical proximity has the effect of taking away some of our inhibitions. The fact that we aren't physically present to our audience means that we are less likely to feel the consequences of our actions. More often than not we don't even know who is receiving the messages we're sending out. We certainly can't pick up the subtle visual clues that individuals give us in a Real Life conversation: the look in the eye that says that a comment has hurt someone or made them feel happy. That can lead people to do and say things online that they wouldn't ever do or say in person.

In 2013 the journalist and feminist campaigner Caroline Criado-Perez led a campaign in the UK to see Jane Austen's picture appearing on the newly designed £10 note. As a result, she started to receive abusive Twitter messages threatening to rape or kill her. Several came from an account with the name @beware0088. The mob effect of Twitter, which can be so useful in spreading news or charity appeals, had the opposite effect. The messages soon became a flood. Scores of people who had never met Ms Criado-Perez nevertheless were able to use the medium to send abuse directly to her phone, copying it to many thousands of other strangers as they did so. Few of her abusers can have stopped to think about the disproportionate impact of receiving such a deluge of completely unwarranted hatred. Some may have been joking, others may have been trying to create an impression among their own followers, and others may simply have been caught up in the moment. But of course the tweets had Real World consequences – genuine distress for Caroline Criado-Perez, a jail sentence for John Nimmo, who was using the @beware0088 Twitter name, and a general but un-measurable coarsening of the public conversation, as equally abusive tweets were sent to others who were tangentially connected to the campaign. The disinhibiting effect of online communication can be similar to the effect of drinking alcohol. It dulls our sense of the consequences of our actions. It loosens our sense of responsibility. Every woman who is in the public eye now knows what it is like to receive messages of hatred from strangers.

It's not true of course that online communications are anonymous. The people who get closest to seeing all my online personas, and who therefore get the richest, fullest, truest picture of me, are not people at all. They are the companies that collect and sort, package and sell all the data I enter through my computer. Even if you set your Facebook account to provide the maximum amount of privacy, so that your updates are seen only by those people you have personally chosen, every keystroke you enter is still recorded by Facebook itself. That's why the company tries to insist that its members use their real names, though Facebook has acknowledged that a total of 8.7% – or 83 million – accounts on the network are bogus. As we have seen, detailed information attached to a name and location is highly valuable to advertisers.

As we shape and project our personalities, we usually assume that we are doing so for the benefit of our friends. But those who want to sell us goods are just as interested in how we see ourselves, if not more so. In response to our disclosure, companies feign a genuine interest in us in return. They get to know us intimately and speak to us in return with a tone that simulates friendship: 'If you like that, you'll like this.' Companies like Amazon take on a faux intimacy because they are projected to us through an intimate object, like a phone or a tablet computer. The fact that they know our interests and preferences so well is subtly flattering. It's seductive. But of course it's ultimately fake. There's nobody home.

We've already seen that the identities we manage are a tiny fraction of the information about us online. Other people tag us in photos, or make comments or whatever. Corporations amortize information to make new info. In any case we 'give off' much more info than we 'give out'. So we have less control than we think.

What's your name?

If we are going to live well in an environment that allows us to play such exotic games with our personality, we will need to have a clear grasp of what we feel is important in human personhood, and what we are prepared to negotiate or trade away in exchange for the joys and benefits of massive connectivity. We'll need to be clear what a healthy person looks like.

The seventeenth-century English philosopher John Locke struggled to pin down what it means to be a person with your own unique identity. He decided that identity wasn't ultimately something that other people recognize in you, but something you know about yourself. For example, Josephine lives in New York. She knows me only through my Twitter account, and not in any other context. Maxine, on the other hand, works in an office in Leeds where she is responsible for my bank account. She doesn't even know that Josephine exists, or that I have a Twitter account. She doesn't care, because she's only interested in my money. Would you say that, because the two people know completely different aspects of me, they actually know two different people? Of course not. It's the same 'me' that sends the tweets and has the overdraft. And by extension it's the same me who has the Facebook page, uses the store card and takes the kids to school. There's only one thing that truly links all of those different personas together, and that is that *I* know they are all me. It's my self-consciousness that, according to John Locke, makes me one person, not many.

Now imagine that in my younger, wilder days I had a Facebook profile on which I uploaded pictures and stories of myself doing younger, wilder things. (Please don't look. Just imagine it!) Years later I live in a different country and I'm starting to look for a job. I wisely decide that that old Facebook history might not be a great recommendation, so I delete the account and open another with a slightly different name and a whole lot more discretion. With luck I might fool a prospective employer. But *I* would always know that the person whose life was recorded in the first account is actually the same person who opened the later, more respectable one. My consciousness of who I am lasts over time and distance. It doesn't depend ultimately on how others see me, but on what I know about myself.

What's true in offline life is just as true in a digital context. However many different personas you might create, project and play with, there's one person who links them all, and that person is you. This has some very important practical consequences. John Nimmo, who persecuted Caroline Criado-Perez on Twitter, might have tried to argue in his defence that he wasn't really responsible for the offending tweets, since they didn't come from him but from his alter ego, @beware0088. But he knew, and the law quickly established, that the person behind the Twitter name should be held responsible for it. The person who sent the tweet is the same person standing in the dock, no matter what name they go by.

Living well requires that I don't behave in one way in private and another in public.

I want to suggest that living well requires that I don't behave in one way in private and another in public – or behave online in ways that I wouldn't behave offline. This matter of the integrity of an individual is a key factor in what makes us human. It's so important that many people would say it is sacred. I am one person, and the embodied me is the root of the genuine me, the me that God and the rest of humanity relates to.

The embodied me is the root of the genuine me.

There's a story in Mark's Gospel in which Jesus encounters a man who is described as being demon-possessed. Jesus asks him his name, and he receives an unexpected answer. 'My name is Legion,' the man says, 'for we are many.' It's an extraordinary phrase. After all, in common usage we assume that every human body is in possession of a single self. If one body has multiple or competing personas that are out of control, we tend to say that person is mentally ill – perhaps schizophrenic.

Lots of Bible commentators have said that the story of Legion is the story of Jesus healing someone who was mentally ill. I'm not so sure. Maybe, in his meeting with Legion, Jesus is signifying a wider truth about the need for us to have an integrity between the embodied person we are and the personalities we express. Maybe the hopeful message of this story is about the potential for healing *dis*-integrated personalities. Through meeting with Jesus, Legion regained 'his right mind' (Mark 5.15). And the integrity he found was so remarkable that according to the writer it was actually frightening to the crowds who saw it.

The integrity of personality is a goal in human wellness. It's fine to express yourself in many different ways in many different places, as long as they all connect back to the real, offline you. But if the digital environment leads us into contradictions or compromises, we're in trouble. If I say to my wife, 'I love you in an offline kind of way', she has every right to get a bit worried. If my Second Life avatar starts sharing stuff with someone else's Second Life avatar that I wouldn't want my vicar to see, that's a problem. That's where Legion had got himself confused. He was afflicted by a muddle of conflicting personalities. To use Sherry Turkle's phrase, he was asking, 'Who am we?' That's why it's so significant that Jesus asked him his name – the only time he did this with anybody. I may be joking away on Twitter, working away on email, chatting away with a friend, loving away in my family; the question is still pertinent: 'Who are you?'

Legion's problems before he met Jesus weren't just psychological but social dis-integration. The crowd didn't know who they were dealing with from one minute to the next. They were scared of him, and they kicked him out. Crowds can do that. That's why bullying is so rife in the online world. And I don't just mean the obvious schoolboy name-calling. There are much more subtle forms of bullying. 'I've got more followers than you have.' 'Share this link or you're not really a good friend.' 'Me and my friends share jokes that you don't even understand.'

The psychologist Erik Erikson observed that for a person to be mentally healthy, not only do they need to have a clear understanding of who they are, but that understanding has to match with who other people think they are. So if I think I'm Brad Pitt's better-looking cousin, but you think I'm ugly, I have a problem. Or if I think I'm a great husband and father, but my wife and children don't, I have a problem. Erik Erikson called that 'an identity crisis'. If he's right, then we need to be careful that the identities we project online are honest and consistent, and that they match up to the reality of who we are in offline life. Online dating sites can be a wonderful way of making contact with people who like the look of you. But many a person using an online dating site has been sadly disappointed when the Adonis in the photo wasn't quite the same as the less than average person who turned up for the first date.

One of the key ways we maintain authenticity is by attaching it to physical bodies. That's partly a recognition that our identities don't only belong to ourselves. They are part of the community. As it happens, I am married. I have the option to create an avatar in Second Life that is unmarried, or to describe myself on Facebook or Tinder as single, or simply to use online spaces to flirt with other people, but I can't do that without impacting my real wife. I'm not sure that it is possible to commit adultery with an avatar, any more than it is possible to steal an object that only exists in a virtual context, but it is certainly possible to behave online in ways that adversely impact people in Real Life. We need to find ways to hang on to the singularity of personality as a goal for living well. We can choose that the people we meet with in embodied personhood – with whom we share houses, streets or bread and wine – will always remain our primary community. Perhaps the answer to the question 'Who am we?' is 'I am many things, but they are all me.'

I am many things, but they are all me.

Pseudonymity

Consider my household electricity bill. Some years ago a meter reader used to visit my house about four times a year and read the meter. He would write the reading beside my name and address, and take it back to an office, where a clerk would calculate my bill and post it to me. There may have been some mechanization in the calculation, and I may never have met the clerk, but the process was essentially human-to-human. In the digital environment the entire contract is mechanized. My digital meter is read remotely by a computer, which attaches the serial number of the meter to my account number. The computer calculates the bill and generates an invoice. Since I have a standing order with my bank to pay the bill, the electricity company's computer automatically exchanges my account number with my bank's computer and the money is transferred. The transaction is notified to me by email, but unfortunately it goes into my 'junk' folder and is automatically deleted! There are human beings working at the electricity company who are eventually paid for their work, and there are human beings in my family who are warmed by the electricity, but everything about the transaction between the two is automated and pseudonymous. The process is convenient and cheap, but the possibility of personal transaction – from offering a cup of tea to the meter reader to pleading for an extension on the payments – is all but lost.

Much of the doctrine of the Internet has suggested that this is a good thing. We are encouraged to treat cyberspace as a dangerous place, and to protect ourselves by carefully hiding our real identity behind a pseudonym. This is unfortunate on several counts. First, as Nancy Baym's research has demonstrated, in most cases people are more, not less honest online than they are in person. Second, in spite of the absence of non-verbal clues on which much human interaction depends, and however hard you might try to disguise your identity online, in many cases people give away far more about themselves than they could possibly control. And third, it is naive to think that just because you use a pseudonym to engage with other users, there isn't a massive collation of meta-information by the owners of websites and ISPs.

An alternative and more holistic approach might be for us all to clearly 'sign' our digital presence; to identify ourselves unmistakably by reference to our embodied self in all our expressions in the digital engagement. If we make digital stuff (blogs, bots, avatars, texts or whatever) that can't be linked to an embodied individual, that diminishes the personhood of the person who made it, and also of the person who receives it. Just think how you feel when you get a text that has an opaque message, and you can't for the life of you work out who it's from. So for instance, even though I use a screen name at my online church (because the program demands it), I make sure that people who meet me there can easily trace me back to my given name. And I make it a rule never to respond to a blog or an email that is written anonymously. As Jesus demonstrated in his encounter with Legion, naming is fundamental to human dignity and to holiness in relationships.

This recognition of the sacred individuality of the human being is the beginning of justice. Similarly in the digital environment, we need to make every effort to retain the humanity of the person who makes content, whether it's a Snap, a blog or a full-length movie, and also the person who consumes it. For me, that means rejecting pseudonymity wherever possible, and making sure that every expression of my digital identity is 'signed' in some way so that it is traceable directly to my embodied

> Our security doesn't come from wearing a digital disguise.

reality. There might be the odd exception, for example where an individual faces a real prospect of bullying or persecution if their identity or whereabouts becomes known. But other than those extreme circumstances, I don't think we should buy the idea that online secrecy produces security, and that safety lies in hiding. That's even true for teenagers. It's easier to bully a person if they are shielded by a pseudonym than it is to be cruel to someone's face. Our security doesn't come from wearing a digital disguise, but from being known.

8

Who Can I Believe?

It was a drizzly November day in 2014 when a little boy approached Pope Francis at one of his regular audiences in The Vatican. The boy was crying, and the kindly Pope asked him why. 'My dog has died,' the little boy said. The Pope smiled at him. 'Don't worry,' he said. 'One day you will see him again in heaven.'

The next day the Italian newspaper *Corriere della Sera* ran a story with the headline 'The Pope and pets: Paradise is open to all creatures'. The story was widely quoted on social media, especially by animal lovers who liked the idea that animals go to heaven. The news spread like wildfire through the religious parts of the digital jungle, as people retweeted it, discussed it on Facebook and so on. Soon, it was picked up by other news outlets, including *The New York Times*, which is read and trusted all over the world. A learned Catholic priest wrote an article for *America* magazine discussing the theological implications of the Pope's comments. It was covered by *The Guardian*, CNN and several doggy magazines. Then the story took a controversial turn as someone noticed that the Pope was contradicting the teaching of his predecessor Pope Benedict XVI who had clearly said that animals don't have souls. The news was taken to be an indication of the new Pope's liberalism and was consequently decried by conservative Catholics. And so it went on.

The trouble is, it wasn't true. Pope Francis had said no such thing. There was no tearful boy and no dead dog. So where had it come from? On the day in question Pope Francis had been preaching to his audience about the environment and quoted from a text in Saint Paul's letter to the Corinthians. It appears that a journalist googled something like Paul + Pope + animals and found a 40-year-old story about Pope Paul VI meeting a grieving boy. Without checking much more than the headline, the journalist attributed the teaching to Pope Francis. He then published it with the headline 'We will go to heaven with the animals' and a picture of Francis with two donkeys. Thanks to the multiplying effect of social media, a simple mistake went around the world posing as a new doctrine. It was aided by the fact that many people wanted to believe it, that Pope Francis was perceived as an animal-lover like his saintly namesake, and probably by the distant memory of an otherwise forgettable cartoon film called *All Dogs Go To Heaven*. If you search the Internet today you can still find scores of sites asserting that Pope Francis has decreed that there are animals in heaven, some of them accompanied by schmaltzy pictures. You can find the quote on T-shirts, fridge magnets and dog blankets. Once the social media dog has got hold of a juicy bone, it never lets go.

In the big picture, accidentally misrepresenting the Pope's views on animals probably doesn't matter too much, but fake news has a darker side. Edgar M. Welch, a 28-year-old Republican father of two from North Carolina, was browsing online when he stumbled on a story that a pizza restaurant in Washington was harbouring young children in its basement and using them as sex slaves. The story said it was part of a child-abuse ring run by US Presidential contender Hillary

Clinton. Welch crosschecked the story, and sure enough the same allegations appeared on other sites including Facebook and Twitter. Mr Welch felt something had to be done, so he drove 400 miles from his home to Washington, where he entered the restaurant and started firing an assault rifle. Fortunately he was restrained before anyone was hurt.

The origins of the story about the restaurant are even more murky than the one about the Pope's love for dogs. It may have been a flight of fancy by an individual, but it could equally have been part of a deliberate campaign of misinformation by a foreign state trying to influence the US election. It may have been left lying around the Internet, or it may have been more precisely targeted at Mr Welch. We've already seen how easy it is for commercial concerns to get to know individuals' personalities and send them subtle marketing messages. It's just as easy for people whose interests are political or religious to use the same techniques to spread information, whether true or false. If anything, governments and political agencies can probably do it on a larger scale. The rumour about the pizza restaurant was clearly nonsense, but it became so deeply rooted that in a poll of over 1,000 Donald Trump supporters 140 said they believed it was true and a further 320 said they were 'not sure'.

It's the 'not sure' people who worry me particularly. They represent a key trend in digital culture that I call a 'learned scepticism'. As we become aware that we are wading through the fog of half-truths and misinformation it's easy to become distrustful of everything. Even without the accidental corruption of truth suffered by the Pope, or the possibly malevolent story about the pizza restaurant (which, incidentally, doesn't have a basement), the nature of information is changing. In the past, the communication of information

The nature of information is changing.

was constrained not only by the time it took, but also by the cost of production. Academics used to have a general rule that if something had been published in book form it probably had a certain level of credibility. A daily publication like *The Times* was regarded as a 'newspaper of record', meaning that it could be counted as an authoritative source by historians. In digital culture, books can be produced quickly and cheaply by just about anybody. Journalists upload their own copy to newspaper websites with barely any checks and balances. The pressure is on to get a story up on the web before your rivals, even if that means cutting a few corners along the way. And that leaves plenty of room for people with political agendas, or people who just want to be anarchic and disruptive. There are allegations that in 2016, during both the 2016 US election campaign and the UK Referendum campaign, overseas governments, particularly Russia, were using hundreds of thousands of bots to influence voters. This is entirely against the election laws of both countries, but it seems almost impossible to identify it, let alone stop it.

Sometimes, fake news is concocted by human individuals. There's nothing new about this. In 1860 a struggling journalist named Theodor Fontane worked as the London correspondent for the *Kreuzzeitung*, a right-leaning newspaper in Berlin. Over a ten-year period Fontane published scores of eyewitness accounts of events in the UK. What his readers didn't realize was that he'd never actually been there. Whenever he heard of something newsworthy happening in Britain, Fontane sifted through other journalists' accounts to get a sense of what readers already knew about the events. He cut up old articles, picked out the most relevant passages, and glued them together for his own story. Then he would add some new passages with details and characters that were completely made up to give the impression he was an eyewitness. Fontane was fooling readers for his own benefit. Others may spread misinformation as a joke, or even just to test how far it will go. I'm sure you are aware that a coati is a small mammal in the racoon family that is found in Central America. If you didn't know that, check it out on Wikipedia. But beware. In July 2008, a 17-year-old student called Dylan Breves edited the Wikipedia article on the coati, saying that coatis are also known as 'Brazilian aardvarks'. They aren't. It was a private joke. There's no such thing as a Brazilian Aardvark. Aardvarks are only found in Southern Africa, not in South America. Nevertheless the article remained uncorrected on Wikipedia for six years. During that time hundreds of websites, academic books and newspapers repeated the 'fact'. In 2010 *The Telegraph* even reported that a small population of Brazilian Aardvarks was living in Cumbria. That report was then cited as a source in the Wikipedia entry, completing the circle of misinformation. The fact that a piece of information is repeated a thousand times on the web doesn't make it a thousand times more likely to be correct.

Sometimes, as in the case of the Pope's views on animal salvation, a story has some basis in truth, but has become changed or exaggerated in the retelling. In a highly competitive culture where 'clicks' are turned into cash, news websites are tempted to deliberately embellish headlines to create 'clickbait' – statements or pictures that entice readers to open a link. The classic formula for this is something like 'Remember X who you used to watch on TV? You'll never guess what she looks like now', or 'Fifteen household objects you've been using wrong all your life.' Who can resist having a look at these items? But be aware that they have been created with the sole purpose of getting you to notice some advertising that sits behind the headline.

What has changed, as with so many aspects of digital culture, is the scale and speed with which misinformation can spread. A bot (or web robot) is a computer program that runs by itself without human intervention. Bots are often designed to act as human beings might in a particular situation, and then set loose on the World Wide Web to do a specific job for their creators. Some of those jobs are beneficial. A bot can be programmed to run on the website of a utility company answering common customer questions, or it may search the train timetables to find the cheapest ticket for you. Those aren't the ones we need to worry about. Many bots are much more harmful. They may buy up all the best tickets for a concert or event, which are then resold at inflated prices by an online ticket tout. That's why some sites have a device asking you to do a sum, or identify some letters, to prove that you are a real human being. Some bots are designed to collect information from websites like Wikipedia and re-present it on different sites, which can in turn sell advertising space. Others visit news sites or online adverts, to artificially inflate the number of people who appear to have viewed them. Advertisers who pay per view on their advert may not realize that up to half the 'visitors' reported to them weren't humans at all.

More worrying still is the rise of bots that are designed to spread unwanted, malicious or untrue messages. Some, known as 'spambots', crawl through the Internet seeking out anything that looks like an email address and harvesting it so that it can be used by a spam marketing company. Others may be programmed to make false accounts on social media platforms such as Twitter or Facebook. Besides artificially increasing the number of friends or followers to a genuine

127

account, they may be used to deliver political or religious messages, or other marketing material. Because they are fully automated they can do this in volumes that are way beyond what human beings could do by themselves.

Ask yourself why a particular message has appeared on the screen of your phone or computer. It could be in the form of an advert, or a tweet, or even something that looks to you like public service information. It appears because someone somewhere, using a very complex set of computer algorithms, decided that it would serve their purposes for you to see it. It may be that they wanted to persuade you to change your mind, to try a new flavour of ice cream or vote for a different political party. To be honest, though, it's really quite difficult to change someone's mind on any of those things. It's much easier to reinforce what we already believe – to make us believe it more strongly or act on it more firmly. Smart advertising doesn't tell us how wrong we are. It tells us we are more right than we had previously imagined. That might mean buying more of the ice cream we've always liked. It might mean committing ourselves more strongly to the political party we already support. Or it might mean pushing us just a little further to the left or the right in our religious or political beliefs. Of course, one tweet or an advert flashing past on a website isn't going to make much difference to our beliefs or behaviour. But if you are presented with a constant stream of messages coming from a variety of different sources over a long period of time, the effect is likely to be quite marked. And if those messages have been targeted at you with the pinpoint accuracy that comes from knowing you better than your closest friend, you will be as vulnerable to persuasive flattery as any of us. In all of this you may not be able to identify what the message is, or who has been funding the advertising. One way to put this right might be for the law to insist that all messages carry some sort of banner or watermark that tells you exactly who paid for the message to be there. That might help – though I can't help thinking that people who are that keen to influence you may be able to find ways of covering their tracks.

It is often suggested that companies that own and manage the architecture of the World Wide Web – companies like Facebook and Google – should take greater responsibility for making sure that what appears on their sites is true. Most companies protest that they are not publishers, but communications providers. They provide a means for other people to communicate, but they can't be held responsible for *what* is communicated, any more than a phone company is responsible for what is said by people using its lines. Facebook, Twitter and YouTube have terms and conditions, which users have to agree to in order to use the service. They have complaints procedures that allow an individual to protest if they feel they are being maligned. They may suspend an account if they judge that it is being abused, but they resist taking any proactive responsibility for determining whether material posted on their sites is true, or defamatory. There are several reasons for this. One is that the sheer volume of traffic makes it unfeasible to police every post or tweet. There have been some attempts to create algorithms that will detect fake news, but so far they aren't very effective. The other reason that digital media companies don't want to take responsibility for policing content is more philosophical. They tend to be wedded to a libertarian approach that says that if there are going to be any limits to free communication, the job of defining them doesn't belong to companies but to individuals, and particularly individuals who are on the receiving end of communications. In short, if you don't like it, don't look at it. Of course communications via social media are subject to the laws of the country in which they are made, so a person who feels that have been defamed or threatened with violence, for instance, may take civil action against the person who made the threat – provided they can identify who that person really was. But that doesn't take account of the huge power of multiplication provided by the networks themselves.

Sometimes the impact of fake news goes way beyond the individual. The average income of a person in Myanmar is equivalent to about £4,000 a year. Most people struggle to meet their basic needs for food and shelter, let alone 'luxuries' like Internet access. And yet in 2017, there were 30 million monthly active Facebook users out of a population in Myanmar of just 50 million. They used a service provided by Facebook known as Free Basics, which gave free Internet access to the majority of people there, while at the same time severely limiting the information available to users. At the time, Facebook offered the same service to the populations of Bolivia, Anguilla, the Republic of Congo and several other impoverished countries. For most people in Myanmar, Facebook was virtually their only source of information online. In 2016 a chain letter began circulating on Facebook in Myanmar. It warned Buddhists that the Rohingya Muslim minority was planning to attack them. A similar letter was sent to Rohingya Muslims warning them to expect attacks from Buddhists. Facebook didn't create the messages, but its site was used to host them. Understandably, suspicion and hatred grew between the two communities in Rakhine State, causing the Muslims to flee the country, with disastrous consequences. The fact that Facebook has since withdrawn its Free Basics service seems to be an acknowledgement that communications companies themselves have some responsibility for what is communicated through their sites.

Are we suffering from truth decay?

'Truth?' shouted Pontius Pilate to Jesus at his trial. 'You can't handle the truth!' Actually, that wasn't Pilate at the trial of Jesus. It was Jack Nicholson in the film *A Few Good Men*. But I don't want to be picky. It was something like that. What does it matter as long as it's roughly the same?

Actually, truth matters a great deal for Christians. In fact, it is probably fair to say that nothing matters more. At his trial Jesus told Pilate: 'The reason I was born and came into the world is to testify to the truth. Everyone on the side of truth listens to me.' And that's a pretty strong endorsement that truth matters. But Pontius Pilate sneered out an answer that wouldn't be out of place in the twenty-first century: 'What *is* truth?'

> Truth matters a great deal for Christians.

In postmodern culture there are several ways of answering Pilate's question, and they can be quite contradictory. At one end of the spectrum is what you might call the 'correspondence' view of truth. That means that truth is an absolute. A statement is true if (and only if) it corresponds to objective reality; to the way things actually are. At the other end of the spectrum there is a view of truth that says that there is no such thing as objective reality. By this understanding it isn't possible to define the way things actually are at all. All truth is relative. A statement can be regarded as true if one or more people agree that it is true. A post box is only red because lots of us agree to call that particular colour by that particular adjective. If we all got together and decided to rename that colour blue, then without anything changing in real life, post boxes would henceforth be described as blue. You can imagine that when it comes to more important matters than the colour of post boxes, the way we understand truth has huge consequences. Is telling a lie objectively wrong … or is it only wrong because we decide it is wrong? Is a creature with two arms, two legs and a head always human … or is that creature only human if the rest of us decide it is? Is a person with two X chromosomes really female … or is there room for discussion?

It is hard to say whether digital culture is a product of postmodernism, or the other way around, but either way, digital communications lend themselves to much more slippery understandings of truth than my grandparents ever had to deal with. When an object can be represented in bytes instead of atoms, it is harder to draw firm lines about what is objectively real and what is not. In my grandparents' day, if a politician had announced that from now on post boxes, clowns' noses and pimples would be described as blue, doctors would soon have taken him away for rest and recovery. Today if a celebrity or a world leader says that black is white or up is down, there's a good chance that many people will start to believe them.

It ought to be simple for Christians to stand up for a 'correspondence' view of truth and say that we will only believe what is objectively factual. The trouble is, Christians (and other people of faith) believe some pretty extraordinary things. If you read the Bible, you may believe that a whale swallowed Jonah. Many believers think that the story recorded in the book of Jonah is objectively, historically, factually true. Maybe it is, maybe it isn't. But it's only a small step from believing that a whale swallowed Jonah, to believing that Jonah swallowed a whale. Most normal twenty-first-century people would find those two scenarios equally difficult to accept. If you want to assert Jonah really was swallowed by a whale, you will need to find some justification for drawing a line between that frankly unlikely story and a lot of other equally unlikely stories like the existence of unicorns or the tooth fairy. If you simply say that the strange stuff that you believe is true because you believe it, while the strange stuff that other people believe is not true because you don't believe it is true, then you have inadvertently adopted a relativist view of truth while you were trying to defend a correspondence view. Many Christians have fallen down that rabbit hole of contradiction, describing things as true primarily because they want to believe them.

That's why notions of truth and falsehood are so important in digital culture. A statement is not true just because we want to believe it. We mustn't describe something as fake news just because we don't agree with it, or don't want to hear it. In an environment that is saturated in information, much of which is amazing or ridiculous or contradictory, who on earth can we trust? How can we know who or what to believe? I wish there was a simple answer to that vitally important question, but there isn't. We all need to learn some of the investigative skills that used to be practised only by journalists. One of the primary attitudes of any good journalist is inquisitiveness – a determination to work out what is true. Another important attitude is scepticism – choosing to allow for the possibility that something that is being presented as truthful may not be. Scepticism is not the same as cynicism (of which journalists are often accused). Cynicism is deciding that everyone is lying, so there's no point in believing anything. Scepticism is consciously and systematically exercising doubt with the aim of getting to what is true. Scepticism can be wise and hopeful. Cynicism was the attitude of Pilate in sending Jesus to the cross.

How to spot fake news ... and avoid creating it

No-one wants to get caught out by fake news, but it looks like a phenomenon that is only going to grow. It is very difficult for governments to counter it – and very tempting for them to exploit it. All of us, as individual consumers of media, need to get smarter about spotting it. When you see a news story in whatever medium, or when you receive an email asking you for money or telling you that you have won something, you need to take responsibility for checking it out.

The first thing to determine is whether you trust the *source* of the story. If you have heard of the organization that published the story or the journalist who supposedly wrote it, that's a good sign. If it is a person or an organization that you trust because they have told the truth before, so much the better. Of course that's not a 100% guarantee of authenticity, because even the best journalists can make mistakes, but credible journalists work in organizations that have lots of editorial checks and balances built into their work. Each news organization has its own standards of fact-checking. BBC News, for instance, normally looks for two independent sources for a story, unless it has come from one of their own correspondents. If a story has made it on to a really authoritative radio or TV station or appeared in a reputable newspaper, that might be a point in its favour. This comes with a caveat. Some newspapers see themselves as more entertainment than news. In 2007, when *The Sun* published a photograph of a Great White Shark swimming off the coast of Cornwall, they already knew it was a hoax. Quite simply, you don't get Great White Sharks in Cornwall. The reporters saw it as a joke and presumably relied on their readers to see it the same way. The traders of Newquay were not so amused, as holidaymakers left the beaches and moved elsewhere for their own safety. The first step to avoiding fake news is to check the source. If you can establish the source of a story, ask yourself what motives there might be for presenting that information to you in that way at this time. Does someone want to sell you something, or persuade you of their opinion, or encourage you to vote for them? Most of us

> The first step to avoiding fake news is to check the source.

develop confidence in particular individuals or brands that we trust to tell us the truth. That's a helpful and inevitable practice. Having said that, it's important not to be naive. If you trust a brand without checking it, you are inviting yourself to be misled. For example, if you automatically believe a news story because it has come from a source that calls itself Christian, or disbelieve it because it comes from a source that describes itself as non-Christian, you may discover that your confidence is misplaced. The Christian doctrine of sin means that the potential for untruth runs like a seam of coal through the whole human race, and Christians are not exempt.

If it is not possible to find out where the story has come from, ask whether the story *sounds* believable. If you read that a zoo has put a dinosaur on display, check the date and see if it is April Fools' Day. Likewise if you are told that you have won a competition you didn't enter, it should start to make you wary. See if you can find the story reported anywhere else. Two news agencies are less likely to be wrong than one. Be careful in this though. A story could appear many times on different websites, but they might all have originated with the same source. Some websites simply collect and re-publish information they have 'scraped' from other websites. A clue to this is the exact repetition of words from one source to another. Just because a piece of information appears in several websites doesn't necessarily make it more reliable.

Look at the website and see whether the news story *looks* normal. Is there anything unusual about the picture? Ask yourself whether this particular image has been selected to make a specific point. Is it possible that it has been digitally manipulated, or re-touched, or simply cropped in a way that tells a particular story that might not be the whole truth? Have the picture and the caption been combined in a way that reinforces a particular stance? Then look at the text itself. Are there spelling or grammatical mistakes in the text that a proper sub-editor would have corrected? Does the website address at the very top of the page look real? If the web address ends with a common domain name such as like '.co.uk' or '.com', that's a good sign. If it ends with something a bit more unusual like '.com.co' you might want to be a bit more cautious. Even the appearance of a website can be a giveaway. Sites that are badly designed, don't fit the screen, or carry logos that look as if they have been cut-and-pasted, are probably not genuine. You can't go laboriously through this process every time you open an email or browse the web. Instead, like wearing a pair of tinted glasses, it needs to become an unconscious attitude of positive scepticism that we all adopt as we encounter information. Sorry – that's the price we pay for having access to vast quantities of unfiltered information.

While it is important not to be taken in by misinformation, it's equally important not to add to the problem. There's always a temptation to retweet or 'like' a piece of information that appeals to me, without stopping to ask myself whether it is true or helpful. The fact that I can pass on a bit of news to many other people with a single twitch of my index finger, and perhaps feel validated in doing so, is a key part of the seductive psychology of digital culture. Pause. Take stock. Check. If in doubt, let it go. Better still, if you see something that is clearly untrue, challenge it. You may not be able to get the genie of fake news back into the bottle of truth, but perhaps you can help a few people to stop and think.

9

Is it Time to CTRL+ALT+DELETE the Church?

One night recently I went to virtual church. Worshipping online is an interesting experience, and you can do it without leaving the comfort of your home. In this particular church, each person was represented by a two-dimensional avatar and a screen name. The program didn't allow me to use my own name, so I chose the name Radioman, and I made sure in my biography that it would be easy for users to connect Radioman with the real me. The church was depicted on screen in quite a traditional way, with a nave, a sanctuary and an adjacent hall. About twenty of us gathered in the church porch before making our way into the worship area. We could communicate with each other by typing words into our computers, which then appeared on the screen for everyone to read. The service consisted of prayers, songs, a Bible reading and a short talk by one of the members.

After the service our avatars all gathered in the bar next door. The advantage of a virtual bar is that it costs nothing to buy everyone a drink. The disadvantage is obvious. As we chatted, we noticed that one person seemed particularly upset, so we asked her what was wrong. It turned out that this lady, who I'd only ever met online, has a young daughter with severe autism. Her condition means that this little girl is sometimes aggressive and often can't sleep – which is all very difficult for my online friend. On this particular night it was all too much and she was very stressed indeed.

This lady and her daughter couldn't easily go to a 'normal' church, partly because her behaviour was so disruptive and partly because it was hard for them to get organized and out of the house at the right time for a Sunday service at her local church. This was a Tuesday evening, and she was grateful to join us via the Internet from her own home. A group of us from the church spent time chatting with her online. We prayed with her, and even tried singing the little girl to sleep, though of course she couldn't actually hear us. It was a really profound and moving moment of the sort that's all too rare in Real Life churches, when there's a real sense of fellowship and mutual support. The strange thing was that of the little group that gathered round, one was in Herefordshire, I was in Manchester, two were in North America and one was in Australia. The lady we were talking to was in Merseyside. It was an entirely virtual meeting, but none the less profound, and the woman at the centre was genuinely encouraged and supported.

To be able to pray with her and support her across thousands of miles was amazing. But I also came away feeling confused. I'd never met the woman we were speaking to in Real Life – in fact I'd only ever met one of the others in the group. We hadn't been able to put our arms around her or even smile at her, except with emoticons. We had sung to the little girl in text, but she hadn't heard us. I didn't know her mother's real name – we were all just pictures and made-up names. In fact for all I know she might not have been a woman, or lived in Merseyside, or had an autistic child at all.

Doing church online is a really strange thing. It has a lot of limitations of course, but it can also take you to places

Doing church online can take you to places that Real Life church seldom goes.

that Real Life church seldom goes. It creates a kind of relationship that is different from anything we've known before. But digital culture also poses real challenges to traditional models of church life. As our understanding of what is 'real' and what is virtual is shaken up by new technology, Christians will need to think about new ways of meeting, organizing ourselves and communicating the gospel. If the Church doesn't adapt to digital culture it will probably last for a while. Like an old analogue TV set it will keep going, looking increasingly old-fashioned but still just about able to function. But eventually the analogue signal will be turned off, and churches, like televisions that haven't been upgraded, will simply be unable to receive programmes and will stop working altogether. Some churches in the West are already finding themselves completely disconnected from the world around them. When my computer gets jammed and refuses to work I sometimes need to switch it off and then on again. If you have a PC you can give it a 'three-fingered salute' by pressing CONTROL+ALT+DELETE. This will dump whatever you were doing and clear the way for a full reboot – a fresh start.

If the Church is to survive, we need to understand how digital technology has changed the culture.

Perhaps it is time to press CONTROL+ALT+DELETE on the Church. This isn't just a matter of changing what a church looks and sounds like – the kind of songs we sing or the ways we speak, or decorate our buildings. It is much more profound than that.

If the Church is to survive, we need to understand how digital technology has changed the culture. We need to be prepared to dump much of what we have been doing and work out what it means to be a church in a digital age.

Far from being redundant, religion and spirituality have a significant place in the digital world. As you might expect, there is a huge diversity of expressions of faith from Adventism to Zoroastrianism. Many churches and other religious communities have used the Internet to extend their ministry. Few people would visit a Real Life church these days without checking out its website first. There are sites dedicated

> Religion and spirituality have a significant place in the digital world.

to evangelism and healing, and sites for people wanting to escape from religion altogether. There are also sites in which people have tried to create entirely new spiritual experiences. In the virtual world known as Second Life, for instance, you will find a digital representation of an Anglican cathedral that looks quite a lot like a Victorian church. There's also a Buddhist temple, a monastery, a mosque, and more esoteric destinations like a Wiccan education centre, several centres of devil worship and The First Church of Elvis.

We've already noted how people use the Internet to design and project personalities into the world. We do that with the religious aspects of ourselves too. Radioman is related to the person I am at my Real Life church Sunday by Sunday, but he is not the same. As we construct our spiritual life online, we draw on offline resources, borrowing language and imagery from offline life.

In my online church there are virtual candles and a stained-glass window, and we mostly use words that you would find in a typical church on the high street. Services have some of the elements of traditional worship, but some things just didn't make the journey from offline to online. It doesn't make sense to kneel in prayer, we can't shake hands to 'pass the peace', and no-one has worked out how to perform sacraments such as baptism and Eucharist when we aren't physically together.

When the images and practices of religion are translated into the online world, their meanings change. A candle emoji has a meaning, but it doesn't have exactly the same meaning as a candle in Real Life. It might provide a good focus for prayer, or you might send it to a friend by text message as a token of encouragement, but it won't provide much light or warmth, you won't be able to play with the wax as it drips down the side and you won't be able to clutch it for comfort. Meanings change and symbols are modified as they move from one medium to another. That's fine, except that if the physical symbols convey things that you believe to be absolutely true, you may feel uncomfortable about the changes. Religious symbols and practices in the digital environment are often used in ways that subvert their original meaning, either accidentally or deliberately. I can point you to a website that will offer to ordain you online for a few dollars, and provide a downloadable certificate to prove it, but that means something different from being ordained by a bishop in a big stone cathedral after several years of study. If ordination isn't important to you, you might see this as trivial – maybe just a bit of a joke – but if ordination is a central part of your religious framework in Real Life, you may be less sanguine about it being devalued. Then, in a post-truth society, who is to say which of those two forms of ordination is really valid? The Anglican Cathedral in Second Life isn't strictly Anglican, nor is it a cathedral, because it doesn't have any official status in the Anglican Communion, but that doesn't stop it operating as a gathering point for worship. Church in digital culture looks very different from analogue church.

In one era and out the other

The arrival of the Internet feels like a revolutionary moment in the communication of Christian truth. Some Christians greet it as a God-given opportunity, while others view it as a threat to all that is holy. It is worth remembering that over the last 2000 years Christian faith has been through a number of communications revolutions, and each time Christians have found ways to adapt to new technologies.

In the very first decades of the Christian Church, technology was limited to hand tools, and the fastest way to travel was by horse. This was the oral era of communication. In ancient Rome, *acta diurna* were used by the government to convey news of military campaigns, trials, executions and edicts. They were chiselled in stone or metal, or sometimes handwritten and read from scrolls by town criers. And of course local news and gossip was passed from one person to another by word of mouth. The effect of this was that there was a kind of intimacy about the transfer of information. You learnt stuff from people you knew, and you could look into the eyes of the person who was speaking and decide whether you trusted what they were telling you. If someone in the community had a reputation for not telling the truth, they would soon be found out. There's something quite democratic about truth being located in personal relationships. We know from studying the ways that the stories about Jesus were transmitted, that far from 'word of mouth' leading to inaccuracy, it could be a very precise means of preserving the truth. If news isn't travelling very far geographically, and it is not 'mediated' through technology, it is relatively easy to crosscheck your sources and work out who and what to believe. One of the most effective ways to pass on information was in the form of stories. When you can't write much down, because not many people can read, truths that are packaged in narrative form are easy to remember.

The first written accounts of the life of Christ were produced within about 40 years of his death. For hundreds of years these early Gospels were copied and passed between churches, sometimes over great distances. The copying process must have been very laborious, and not many ordinary people could write or read, so word of mouth was still important. It's sobering to think that, for almost three-quarters of the history of the Church, this is the fragile and labour-intensive way in which the good news of Jesus has passed from one person to the next.

Then, around 1440, Johannes Gutenberg developed a means of printing using moveable type. In the following decades the world entered a new era of communication. In this literary phase, those people who owned or controlled a printing press had immense power over communication. One person's ideas, in a book or a newspaper, could reach and influence thousands of others. Right up to the twentieth century books were rare enough and expensive enough that they carried a special authority. Academic convention said that if information had been published in a book it was probably worth noting. Until the arrival of the paperback at the start of the twentieth century, writing, printing, owning and reading books was largely the domain of the wealthy elite. One effect of that was to give some people great power over other people's access to reliable information. Control of information went alongside accessibility. The Church was just one of the institutions to exploit that opportunity, making the Bible and other Christian writings widely available, but only to those who had enough education to read and understand them.

The nature of the print medium had an impact on

the way that information could be presented. Books are particularly good for recording information in a linear way. You tend to start at the beginning and read to the end, so they work for telling stories, but they also do a good job of expressing lines of argument that need to be carefully developed. Books can be used to present truth in the form of ideas and propositions. As the Church committed more and more of its teachings to written rather than oral form, so its teachers began to think and speak more about doctrines and reasoning rather than about stories.

The literary form of transmission suited the leaders of the Church so well that in many ways they have never left it. We are entering the digital era with a Church that is still highly dependent on books, and has grown used to expressing the gospel in propositional terms. If you ask most Christians to give you a summary of the good news, they won't tell you a story; they will give you a formula. But while the Church has stayed comfortable in the literary era, the rest of the world underwent a communications transformation even bigger than the invention of the printing press.

There's a long-running dispute as to who was the first company to offer broadcasting to the masses. The British Broadcasting Company launched its first domestic radio service in 1922 under the leadership of its first Director-General John Reith, a dour Scottish Presbyterian with an uncomfortable admiration for Hitler. It took another ten years for the renamed British Broadcasting Corporation to start transmitting internationally. Meanwhile in 1931 Vatican Radio, under the personal direction of Guillermo Marconi, started broadcasting on short wave in 47 languages. Whichever of the two was first, the advent of radio changed everything for religious communication.

It wasn't until the 1940s that the dynamics of information

control began to change rapidly. With the invention of broadcasting, the cost of producing information stayed high, so it was still restricted to an elite. But the cost of receiving information was very low. The numbers of people listening to a radio programme or watching a TV show was huge. One of John Reith's first actions as Director-General of the BBC was to invite the then Archbishop of Canterbury Randall Davidson to his London flat to demonstrate how a radio receiver worked. As they sat down to dinner the BBC was playing a particularly vigorous orchestral piece by Tchaikovsky. The Archbishop commented that it was a rather intrusive piece to listen to during a meal. John Reith picked up the phone to the studio and instructed them to put some soothing piano music on instead. Many religious leaders since then might have wished they had some of Reith's power or Davidson's influence over the media.

You might have thought that the Church would be quick to jump on the broadcasting bandwagon. Instead, in the intervening decades, religion and media have engaged in an uneasy stand-off. Almost all communities of religion and belief complain regularly about being misrepresented, under-represented or occasionally mistreated by the media. In truth there are misunderstandings on both sides. Broadcasting lent itself to communicating stories better than ideas, and religious leaders had largely forgotten how to speak in ways that non-academics could understand.

Before the advent of broadcasting, the Church had significant power to host the public conversation. Broadly speaking it was the Church that told people how to behave, what to wear, who was important, and what was going on in the community. Today it is the mass media that assumes those privileges. For example, in pre-broadcast generations, the liturgical calendar marked out the year. It was Advent, then Christmas; Lent, then Easter. Today the media have their own liturgical calendar. It's autumn, so it's *Comic Relief*. *Strictly* is on – it must be nearly Christmas. Summer is here – the *X Factor* season. The wide choice of content that became available meant that religious and political ideas have to jostle with news and entertainment, music and drama, for the attention of the audience. It's the media, not the Church, that now has ability to 'change the weather' in terms of the meta-narrative of society.

At the end of the twentieth century, while the Church was still trying to come to terms with the arrival of broadcasting, the dynamic changed again. Web 2.0 introduced a many-to-many communications culture. For the first time since the oral era, the person speaking and the person listening had roughly similar authority. Digital communication is still better at stories and pictures than ideas, but the level of choice is now overwhelming.

It has been said that the Internet is the car boot sale of the soul. There's more stuff to see than there is time to see it, but only some of it is valuable. If I look at my browser history for yesterday, for example, it tells a story of random connections and unknown consequences. I see that I visited a train booking site, a political party, a friend's blog, a story, two social networks that I belong too, a wiki … and so on. I seem to have spent my day hopping from

> The Internet is the car boot sale of the soul.

site to site, subject to subject, like a bee tasting pollen at a thousand flowers. The web is incredibly useful. I don't know quite how I managed without it. But I tend to engage with subjects at a shallow level, and certainly not in the depth that reading a book demands. My browser history looks a bit like a dream, with images and stories crashing into each other. I'm not untypical. How can I or anyone else make sense of this mosaic of unsifted fragments? Is there simply too much information?

Christians who have grown up primarily with literary models may find it hard to adjust to new modes of communication. Like Hamlet, we are fearful of dreams. They feel out of control. But dreaming has a good pedigree in the Bible. God spoke to Abraham, Jacob and Daniel in dreams, and to Joseph, Peter and Paul. There's no reason why God shouldn't use digital media to speak today. We need to get clever about how we use it though. If you look back at my browser history from yesterday you will see that it jumps wildly between genres. One minute I'm looking at some facts (the train timetable), the next I'm looking at some informed speculation (the weather), then I move to comment (my friend's blog) and fiction (the story) and so on. We need to be aware what genre of information we are looking at. If we mistake comment for fact, or fiction for speculation, we will soon become confused, and then potentially pass our confusion on to others. Christians ought to be good at this, because we have to do the same thing when we read the Bible, hopping from history to speculation, and from poetry to fiction.

Opportunities

When I was a young Christian, missionaries had to go to great lengths to take the message of the gospel to far-flung parts of the world. One particular missionary society used to send representatives to visit our church and speak about their work. They had erected a radio mast in The Seychelles, which they used to broadcast evangelistic programmes into parts of the Far East that were closed to Christian missionaries. Today, with over half of the world's population connected via the Internet, making contact with people is much easier (although governments in some parts of the world still don't allow their populations freedom to access external content). The bigger question is how to present the Christian message in digital culture.

In some ways communicating in digital culture is quite like communicating in the story-telling era. When you 'speak' online you are addressing an audience of one. That one individual, reading or listening through a tablet or a laptop, may be multiplied many times over, but they receive the information as an individual. The Internet has enabled individuals to meet one another across the boundaries of space and time. The communications don't come with the implied authority of a physical book or a TV programme. The weight that the receiver places on the message will depend entirely on their relationship with the individual who sent it. The upside of this for Christians is that we have an amazing opportunity to communicate with individuals all over the world, without the need for a printing press or a radio transmission mast. The downside is that what we say no longer carries the added credibility that used to come from publishing and broadcasting. The fact that you are the professor of something or the archdeacon of somewhere no longer gives you an automatic authority. After all, I can be ordained online in my coffee break if I so choose. In digital culture, powerful communication depends on authenticity.

> In digital culture, powerful communication depends on authenticity.

All of this is a challenge to the ways in which the Church has traditionally distributed authority. We're no longer inclined to believe something is true just because the person who said it was wearing a big hat or had a university degree. Believers and doubters have virtually unrestricted access to ideas and information. When a politician has made a speech or a pastor has preached her sermon, there's every opportunity for the audience or congregation to check the facts, and to compare what they have heard with what others are saying. The Christian community will have to come to terms with new forms of authority, and Christian leaders will have to get used to a great deal less deference to their position. There is no Archbishop of the Internet. Instead, we all have to work out who we trust, and who we want to follow, on the basis of the recommendations of our friends and the authenticity we discern in the messengers. The traditional structures of authority in churches have been very comfortable for those who became leaders, but they have also been comforting for those who wanted to be led. There is a certain security in someone with a good education and a title before his name telling you what to do. One of the challenges of digital culture will be to design and build Christian communities that are much flatter.

Image

When I went to church as a child, I was encouraged to take a Bible along with me. Almost every church service I have ever been to has been shaped and formed around words – the words of Scripture and prayers expressed in words. It's not for nothing that Christians often described themselves (alongside Jews and sometimes Muslims) as 'People of the Book'. What they mean is that the roots of authority in those faiths grow out of sacred texts, in the form of words on a page.

The first websites looked a lot like academic journals. They were full of words with very little illustration. That was partly because users still had to dial a phone line to access information. It was slow to arrive and expensive, so the content was presented in a form that took the minimum time to download. In due course the price of Internet access dropped and download speeds increased. Designers started to add images to the plain text, so that websites took on the form of a magazine with pages broken up by pictures. To be honest, pornography was one of the main driving forces in this new way of using the web. As downloads became even faster, web designers started to add moving images and sound to their pages. Very often, if you wanted to see the movie, you had to wait while it downloaded. Eventually, with the advent of broadband technology, it became possible for most people to download video pictures in 'real time'. In other words, you no longer had to wait while the pictures were 'buffering'. A Rubicon had been crossed. It was practical to upload short videos and download long ones. From that point on, moving images were the norm for web design. Advertisers (and of course pornographers) were delighted by this development.

'The People of the Book' now find themselves operating in the culture of the moving image, and that poses some significant challenges. How crucial is it that the Christian story is expressed in words in a book made out of a dead tree? Of course it is possible to be a Christian, even if you can't read or write. In fact the majority of Christians through the ages have had no direct access to printed Bibles or other books. But many Christians have come to see the study of words on a page as central to their Christian experience. The Word became flesh in the incarnation of Jesus, but the Church has spent hundreds of years turning the flesh back into words. The Church has come to rely heavily on text, and it will have a momentous shift to make if it is to find ways of expressing faith primarily in pictures and moving images.

It may be best to think of the past six hundred years as an aberration in the history of the Church. Before the arrival of print and broadcasting, the gospel was passed on from one individual to another, largely expressed in images and stories. Jesus didn't teach his disciples in a linear, propositional way, but through eye-catching pictures and memorable tales, all delivered in the context of close relationship. Perhaps we shouldn't worry too much about controlling the 'grand narrative' of the gospel's teaching, but should retrain ourselves to express the good news in tweet-sized fragments – unconnected jigsaw pieces that resonate with everyday experience and catch in the heart. The average length of time a viewer sticks with a YouTube video is just two minutes. Then they are off to something else. You can't develop much of an argument in two minutes, but if you are smart you can tell a good story.

The downside of treating the gospel in this way is that we lose the sense of the grand story of God's activity in the world. In the days when I carried my big blue Bible to church the preacher would call out the Bible readings and, if we were lucky, give out a page number. Since the Bible is arranged in roughly chronological order it was relatively simple to work out where one particular passage of Scripture fitted into the whole narrative. A Bible passage that is projected onto a screen or downloaded from the Internet comes without a context. We will have to find ways of setting individual images and stories into the bigger narrative. We need movies as well as ad-length downloads to tell the story in pictures.

The Church of St Wherever

One evening a couple of years ago I joined with a group of friends to worship at the Anglican Cathedral in the virtual environment of Second Life. Watching on a big screen in Durham, we joined in worship with people from all over the world, all represented by their avatars in a virtual church.

It was inspiring, but also confusing. The worshippers were located in many different time zones, so for some it was Morning Prayer but for others it was Evensong. And while I was in northern England, the service was being led by someone in New Zealand, and the server that was hosting the program was in California. The Bishop of Durham happened to be with us in our live congregation, but when I asked him whether his episcopacy covered this particular service he couldn't answer me.

When the Church began, almost 2000 years ago, the question of which particular congregation you would join was not an issue. You were part of whichever church met in your town, or within walking distance of your house. On the whole it stayed that way for over 1000 years. Choosing a church was not a matter of market forces but ease of travel. The New Testament foundations of the Church were based on a geographical model – the church that meets in my town. That's why the epistles of Paul in the New Testament are named after the towns to which they were directed – Ephesus, Corinth and Thessaloniki. Much later as transport developed you could attend whichever church you could ride to, or drive to. Still churches were defined by geography. Today, most churches have a place name somewhere in their title: St George's Edgware, or St Nicholas Durham. It made sense to arrange the leadership of the Church in geographical ways too. Clergy were appointed to places, and bishoprics were named after larger geographical areas. The Church of England even divided the whole country into parishes, so that for many years every location was related to a particular church with its own priest. In theory at least, the religious community you belonged to was determined by the place where you lived.

Digital culture changes all that. Online communities

form around shared interests rather than shared geography. If I wanted to, I could worship with a group of bald-headed overweight Stockport County supporters like myself. We might not be much of a church, but we could probably find enough for a small house group. We have yet to discover how the nature of church changes when it is linked by something

Online communities form around shared interests rather than shared geography.

other than place. And we've got a great deal to work out about how to do church with people with whom we are not physically present. At first it may seem unthinkable – but then

I used to keep my money in a bank on my local high street, where I could go in and ask the man behind the counter for cash. The bank that looks after my money today doesn't have any branches at all, and I've never met anyone who works for it. I've never met my bank manager and that's OK. Will it be OK if I never meet my vicar either?

The fact that for 2000 years the Church has been geographically based is more than just a matter of convenience. It raises a profound question about where God lives in the world. Jesus said that where two or three people were gathered in his name, he would be present with them, but it's not at all clear whether gathering in his name depends on the actual clash of bodies in a physical place, or whether other sorts of gathering might do the same job. If we say that any kind of meeting, including the kind of meeting that can take place online, is enough for Jesus to be present, we risk devaluing the actual physical coming together that the first disciples experienced when they met in the Upper Room and Jesus joined them. But if we say that Christ is not present when Christians meet virtually, we ignore the very real fellowship that can be found across miles and even outside of time.

Opinion is divided as to whether it makes any sense to share sacraments such as communion and baptism in a virtual world. It is possible to enact a Eucharist in an online church, in the sense that an avatar could receive digital representations of bread and wine. Since the whole digital world is part of God's creation, it makes sense to say that God is present in digital spaces too. And although an avatar couldn't receive any benefit from communion because it isn't conscious, it's quite likely that the person controlling that avatar might be blessed by the experience. And yet a great deal of the potency of sacraments lies in their physicality. The experience of being fed in communion or washed in baptism involves all of the senses. You can smell and touch and taste and see and hear the tearing of bread, the pouring of wine and the splashing of water. Sacraments are symbols of God in action in the world. There's no doubt that God can act in and through a simulated, virtual world if God chose to do so. The deficit would be on our end, not God's. Symbols are much less powerful if they come to us without the correlate physical sensations. When I shake hands with my neighbour in church during the Passing of the Peace, the brushing of our palms or the slap on the back means more than just the words we exchange. At this point in our church service, after I have greeted the people around me, I always quietly take out my phone and share the peace by text with a friend of mine whose illness means she can't leave her bed. I would rather give her a friendly hug, but she lives three hundred miles away from me. In fact we've never met in person. The texted exchange of peace goes some way to including her in the life of my local church – which she's never been to in person either. It's not enough, but it means something. I still hope that we will meet one day face to face. The author of the Letter to the Hebrews urged his readers not to give up the habit of meeting together (Hebrews 10.25). There are lots of ways of meeting together, but the most important ones require us to be in the same place and time. In an age when so much of our communication takes place in disembodied forms, many people crave the greater integrity and deeper relationships that come packaged in a human body. The church – the old-fashioned church offering uncomfortable seats in a draughty building at inconvenient times – is in a unique place to provide this. The simple embodiment of fellowship might turn out be one of the greatest missional tools of the twenty-first century.

10

Is My Body Due for an Upgrade?

Digital culture is full of surprises. For many years now anyone equipped with a laptop or a mobile phone has been able to access a bewildering range of pornographic videos, and watch strangers having unfeasibly satisfying sex. Men and women have used these images to get turned on, just as our parents used glossy magazines and our grandparents used What The Butler Saw machines. But until fairly recently most of us assumed that in order to actually have sex you needed at least two people, and they had to be in the same room at the same time. Not any more.

In recent years a new range of haptic sex toys known as teledildonics has been developed. A teledildonic set consists of two pieces of equipment, roughly shaped like male and female genitals. These devices can be plugged into a computer (or linked wirelessly) so that the users can transmit feelings over the Internet as easily as making a conventional phone call. Link them with pictures on the screen and two people can stimulate each other sexually, even though they are miles apart. A student can have something like sex with their girlfriend or boyfriend even if they are at the other end of the country. Prisoners or soldiers on active service can have sex across the miles. Digital sex toys have swept away the need for two people to be in the same place to have a sexual encounter. The devices are fairly crude at the moment – in both senses of the word – but as the technology advances, the sensations they transmit will become more and more lifelike.

Internet-enabled sex toys can break the bounds of time as well as space. Once you have got used to the idea of having sex (or something like it) using a machine, the possibilities are endless. If you don't have a partner to have sex with, perhaps you could download a sexual experience from the web. You could customize your sex partner or buy a pre-programmed interactive package of sex with your favourite film star. You could use the best and worst of your imagination to create virtual sexual partners, real or imagined, human or otherwise. You could record and repeat your greatest sexual experiences. You could simulate sex with multiple partners at the same time. You could even store up sexual experiences you have enjoyed with your partner during life and relive them after their death.

If you think this is far-fetched, let me remind you how much the development of the Internet has been driven by the availability of pornography. SexTech, as it is known, is a multi-billion-dollar industry continually looking for the next business opportunity. Already there are companies marketing robotic sex dolls in full-size humanoid form. They have flesh-like synthetic skin and false hair. They have limited mechanical movements, and sensors that can respond to voice commands. They are pre-programmed with characteristics you choose – shy, flirty, submissive … literally whatever turns you on. In the vast majority of cases the doll has the body-shape and voice of a girl between puberty and mid-20s, though male and child sex robots are also in construction.

Some people see sex dolls as more than just a business opportunity. They suggest that they could have a real role in sex education, or that they could provide comfort for people who are prevented from having sex by their disability or other circumstances. Others even feel that providing childlike sex dolls to paedophiles might help them to overcome or restrain their perverse sexual desires without harming actual children, a little like giving methadone to a heroin addict. Maybe this is not for you. But for some people, sex with a robot, in whatever form that takes, may look like a way to deal with their hunger for intimacy. Certainly it is more reliable than conventional sex. There is no risk that a machine will reject you, or give you a disease, or make you pregnant. The Futurologist Dr Ian Pearson has said that in the future, 'sex will be easier, safer, more frequent and a lot more fun'. He means sex between a human and a machine.

Up to now, sex robots are more an idea than a reality. Even after years of research and development, humanoid sex robots are still extremely crude devices, unable to reproduce rather basic features of the human body like temperature, moisture and scent. The instance most frequently cited in the media is Roxxxy TrueCompanion, a latex gynoid produced by inventor Douglas Hines, which has been the subject of hundreds of articles and documentaries since it was first announced in 2010. Roxxxy is marketed online for $9,995 and has allegedly been pre-ordered by thousands of men around the world. Curiously, not a single instance of Roxxxy has been seen outside Hines' workshop. The few images you see in magazine articles are barely distinguishable from the sort of inflatable sex toy that has been widely available since the 1950s. There is no published research on partners' experience with Roxxxy. In short, Roxxxy probably doesn't exist except as a prototype, and sex robots are probably not much more than a thought experiment. The degree of breathless interest in humanoid sex robots tells us more about ourselves, and the ways we think about sex and technology, than it does about the objects themselves.

My own guess is that full-spec sex robots like the ones you see in the movies will never really catch on. The technology is too clunky and the cost is too high. Instead I expect the gap to be filled by virtual reality, which does most of the same job. Slip on a VR headset, download an app, and you can have an immersive sexual experience where you feel as if you are at the centre of the action, choosing your own angles and coming and going as you please with a 3D representation of your own partner, or whoever else you choose. Add a simple haptic device and the experience will be 'real enough' for most users. That kind of equipment is not far-fetched. It's only a step away from video pornography as we know it. Bear in mind that, with the almost ubiquitous availability of online sex sites, sex between two people is already far less common than sex between one person and a machine of some sort. In due course we may be able to make a direct connection between a computer program and the nervous system, to stimulate the brain directly, rather than through the skin or the eyes, and then we could bypass the need for pictures and sounds altogether. If you need a little break at this point to take all this in, feel free to stop for a nice cup of tea.

Sex with some*one* or sex with some*thing*?

It's all too easy to reject new technologies simply on the basis that they feel uncomfortable or a bit creepy. Sexual relationships are often fraught with difficulties. Some are exploitative, and some are disappointing. At least in a relationship between a person and a machine no-one gets harmed or abused or let down. A machine can't get pregnant either, or catch a sexually transmitted disease. Perhaps we should see machine sex as a morally neutral form of sexual expression – no better or worse than using a kettle to make a nice cup of tea. People have been using objects and potions for sexual stimulation for thousands of years. If we want to decide whether or not it is OK to have sex with a robot, or a computer, or

> It's easy to reject new technologies simply on the basis that they feel uncomfortable or a bit creepy.

any machine for that matter, we'll need a better reason than 'because it doesn't feel right'. There's no doubt that you can have something like sex with something like a person. But I think that's setting your sights very low. I'm a firm believer that the best sex happens between two people in the same place at the same time.

One of the supposed advantages of sex with a robot is the degree of control the user can exercise over the experience. TrueCompanion's Roxxxy is advertised as 'always turned on and ready to talk or play'. The best sex involves two people who approach it on equal terms. In making love, each partner affirms the value and dignity of the other as equal to their own. That's why we tend to think that sex between unequal partners such as an adult and a child, or a human and an animal, is taboo. That's why many people believe that sex between a client and a sex worker is wrong too, although some feel that paying or being paid can redress the balance of power. Good sex is basically symmetrical. The primary way that we guarantee that sex is just is by consent. Consent creates affirmation – a willing suspension of the power balance between two people that means they view the act of sex as a joint creation. That's why we sometimes call it 'making love'. Person-to-person sex involves mutual vulnerability, giving up control to another. There's something sacred about two people agreeing to make themselves that defenceless to each other, and it can have a powerful effect. Mutual vulnerability can help to build a relationship. In many cases the possibility of having a baby together is part of the creative impulse released by good consensual sex.

The trouble is, a machine can't consent to sex. On the plus side, that means that a machine can't come to any harm through having sex with a human, but on the minus side, the human can't really experience the power of intimacy to strengthen or heal the bond. The reverse might be true, however. A person whose partner has sex with a robot might feel as if they were cheating. So sex with a machine could damage an existing relationship, or make a person feel inadequate. Not all human-to-human sex includes the possibility of having a baby, but it always includes the possibility of rejection; of feeling hurt or disappointed. Strangely enough, the imperfection is part of what makes human sex so powerful. When we have sex with a person we are saying: 'I am willing to be vulnerable with you. I am willing to risk getting hurt.' The very fact that robot sex is risk-free makes it less valuable than human sex.

If you order a sex robot it will be made to your exact specifications, with the eye colour, hips, breasts and hairstyle you prefer. You may be charged extra for some characteristics if they are more specialized or use more latex to construct, but if you like, you can have a second doll made exactly the same in case you lose the first one. In contrast, if you have sex with a human being, you will find they are not so perfect. And I'm sorry to tell you, but you will find you aren't so perfect either. The good news is that every human body is unique, and because

> Every human body is unique, and because each person is unique, it is impossible to put a price on them.

each person is unique, it is impossible to put a price on them, and impossible to find one just the same. What you might see as imperfections are part of what makes that person irreplaceable, and accepting them (and having your own quirks and foibles accepted) is a large part of the affirmative power of human sex. The bottom line is, a robot can probably stimulate you to orgasm, but it won't make you feel any better about yourself.

All of this assumes that you are aware that you are having sex with a robot, not a human. As things stand at the moment the difference between a person and a machine is usually pretty obvious, but one of the goals that technologists have always aimed for is to make machines that are indistinguishable from people. Making a machine that *looks* and *feels* like a human is quite difficult but making a machine that *behaves* like a human being is not. All it takes is more and more computer memory and some sophisticated mechanics. If you want to make a machine that looks as if it is experiencing pleasure or pain or jealousy, for instance, you can watch lots and lots of people who are experiencing those emotions, and record in intense detail how they behave. Once you have gathered the data you simply program your machine to do exactly what a human would do in those circumstances. Our ability to do this is getting better all the time. When the first voice simulators were made, they sounded very mechanical, so it was easy to tell they were not 'real'. They couldn't accurately copy the inflections of a human voice, and they never paused or stumbled as we do in normal speech. Now, though, some voice synthesizers can imitate the human voice with such accuracy, including the ums, errs and pauses, that it is virtually impossible to say which is a computer and which is a person. A machine can never feel love or jealousy or anger, but with enough data to learn from it can be made to *look* as if it feels any or all of those things.

The sextech industry is quick to exploit those advances. Roxxxy comes 'pre-loaded with five separate girlfriend personalities' including 'Frigid Farah – she is reserved and shy; Wild Wendy – she is outgoing and adventurous; S and M Susan – she is ready to provide your pain/pleasure fantasies.' Characteristics that might be seen as fundamental to personhood are reduced in the robot to a series of mechanical responses that are analogies of the response a human might make.

Such analogies can only work by reducing characteristics – boiling them down to basics. Early sex robots offer a highly selective and objectified approach to what it means to have a body and to enjoy sexual pleasure. In the vast majority of cases the machine-partner is construed as a physically idealized white (or sometimes Asian) female. They are designed with an emphasis on the sexual organs; the breasts, lips, genitals and anus. Dolls and their body parts aren't realistic, because real bodies are full of quirks and imperfections. Sex dolls are not anatomically accurate, but anatomically reductive. They are idealized, with hair colour, breast size and other features modified to match the preferences of the user. So although some bioethicists like Ezio Di Nucci want to suggest that the sexual satisfaction of physically and mentally disabled people could be fulfilled by deploying sex robots, in reality those people are unlikely to find robots that have their own untypical bodily forms and behaviours.

It is possible to imagine a highly anatomically accurate reproduction of a human body, but it turns out that anatomically accurate is not what we want. Sculptors in Ancient Greece tried to make idealized statues, not accurate ones, and today's technologists have a similar aim. But there's a hitch. Research has shown that as technologists make robots that are more and more like a real human, there comes a point where we stop saying 'Wow' and instead say 'Yuck'. They have a name for it. It is called 'The Uncanny Valley'. It seems that we humans find it disturbing to engage with something that is *almost* like us but not quite. We would rather settle for something that is just alike enough to do the job we want done. In the case of sex robots, it seems that in most cases the goal is a male orgasm. Whatever equipment you produce doesn't need to be perfect. It just needs to be good enough to make a man orgasm. Real sex is not nearly so simple. Real sex is more than just orgasms. If it weren't, we could probably just engineer a pill that would make an orgasm happen, and do away with the risky, sweaty business of sex altogether. Real sex is a whole person activity, in which body and mind are fully wrapped up together, and the motor driving it is the desire that two people share for the other one to be happy and affirmed. It's not just about looking for happy feelings for yourself but making a free choice to look for happy feelings for someone else. A robot might make you feel good, but that's a pretty diminished, one-sided sort of sex. Once again, it's an example of human beings limiting ourselves to accommodate the limitations of machines.

You can't make a robot feel anything at all. Robots don't feel. They just act as if they do. You could argue, then, that sex with a robot is OK, because it doesn't do anyone any harm. That might be true, except that if we get into the habit of treating things as if they were people, we run the risk of starting to treat people as if they were things. For our own wellbeing and dignity, and for the cohesion of our communities, we need to keep a clear demarcation line between people and things. Professor Simon Baron-Cohen

Robots don't feel. They just act as if they do.

165

is a psychologist specializing in autistic spectrum disorders. He argues that lack of genuine empathy underlies much of human cruelty, a cruelty he describes as people turning people into objects, a process that changes us over time so that in the end we relate only to things, or to people as if they were just things. Paedophiles are a classic case of blurring the line between people and things. Give a paedophile a childlike sex robot and they may just get used to the idea that you can have sex with anyone or anything and they won't get hurt. To have real sex needs two real people.

> To have real sex needs two real people.

When his wife died, C. S. Lewis recorded his feelings and reflections in a book called *A Grief Observed.* He wrote: 'The most precious gift that marriage gave me was the constant impact of something very close and intimate, yet all the time unmistakably other, resistant – in a word, real.' Sex, alongside physical illness, is probably the experience that makes us most conscious of our embodiedness. This is the 'becoming flesh' part of the biblical notion of two people becoming one flesh. At the same time as we become aware of the physicality of the other person, we also become aware that, however much we would like to be merged with the other person, it isn't going to happen. The more we try to make two people become one person, the more we realize it can't happen. Two bodies can't occupy the same space simultaneously. That's the tragedy of sex. It forces us to realize that our closest friend will always be a stranger.

Human 2.0

Come with me on a little 'thought experiment'.

If a short-sighted person wears glasses to help them to see better, do you have any objection? I'm pretty sure the answer is no. Short sight is a nuisance, and if all you have to do to overcome it is to put a carefully calibrated piece of plastic on your nose, no-one's going to object. So far, so good. What about contact lenses? Any problems there? No. I didn't think so. Not everybody gets on well with contact lenses, but if you do, good for you. Let's take it to the next step. How do you feel about laser eye surgery – where a skilled ophthalmologist uses a laser beam to reshape the cornea on the front of your eyeball? It can be a safe and effective way of correcting short sight, long sight and astigmatism. Is that OK? Well, there's a bit of a yuck factor about a surgeon burning lines into your eyeball, but broadly speaking most of us don't have a moral problem with it. All of these techniques – glasses, contact lenses and laser eye surgery – use widely available technology to correct a defect to bring a person's failing eyesight back to normal. None of them fundamentally changes a person's body or takes away anything that was there before. Fair dos.

Now let's take it a step further. Supposing scientists developed a tiny camera that could be inserted into a human eye socket, that would give the person who had it far better eyesight than your normal eye. It would transmit pictures directly into the human brain. It would enable the person who had it to see miles into the distance, or it could be adjusted to use as an embedded microscope, seeing the world in tiny detail. Maybe it's so clever that you could even use this mechanical eyeball to see in the dark, or look round corners, or to see X-ray pictures. That would be particularly helpful to soldiers on the battlefield. If you could have such an amazing piece of technology fitted, would you do it? Would that be OK? And would you have any moral objection if, in order to use this super-eye, a person had to have their own eyeball removed? I wonder.

If a person had been born blind it would seem quite appropriate to use technology to give them the ability to see, just as we give hearing aids to people who are deaf to enable them to hear. We might have to remove their non-functioning eyeball for this to happen, and that's a distasteful idea, but it's no worse than amputating a diseased leg in order to fit a prosthetic one. What if the aim of the technology was not to correct a defect, but to enable the body to do something it couldn't do before? Many of us instinctively draw a line between restoring a defect to bring a person back to normality, and doing something that enhances a body, to give them a technological advantage. We think it's fine to take Paracetamol to make a headache go away, but we think it's wrong for a weightlifter to take steroids to help them win a gold medal. We think it's OK for a person who loses their legs to use a wheelchair, even a motorized one, but we might draw the line if that wheelchair could do 40 miles per hour. We're happy for a Paralympic athlete to run on steel blades, but if those steel blades are fitted with a mechanical device to make them go faster, we call that cheating.

In digital culture, questions about how far we should improve the human body have moved to a new level. For the first time we can combine our 'natural' bodies with technology that enables them to do things that were previously unimaginable. We can implant chips under our skin, and exchange body parts made of skin and bones for more powerful tools manufactured, programmed or grown in a laboratory. A combination of a human body and a piece of digital technology is known as a cyborg. This step-change in our ability to enhance human bodies forces us to ask hard questions about soft tissue. What, if any, are the limits to human improvement?

For many years, technologists have challenged themselves to create a machine that acts and reacts in every way like a biological human being. It hasn't yet proved possible to manufacture a single object that does everything a human body can do, but if you break down the parts of a body into separate functions, a good many can already be done better by a machine. Robots can perform complex operations with more precision than a surgeon's hand could ever manage. Computers can make calculations that are so complex no individual brain could attempt them. Digital telescopes and microscopes can see further or smaller than the human eye ever could. Perhaps it will one day be possible to combine all of these advantages and create a machine that does everything that humans can do, only better. All of this forces us to ask whether there is something sacred about human beings as we know them, or whether we should regard the present state of human evolution as just a stage of development that can and will be superseded. Some might argue that it's arrogance driven by superstition that leads us to believe that human beings are the pinnacle of anything. We should just get over ourselves. After all, they say, it is an ethical imperative to improve human life and make the world a better place. Why wouldn't we? We already do. If someone has a deficiency, we seek to make it up to a norm. We value education to improve our minds and exercise to improve our bodies. Why not go further and use technology to improve our species? The Astronomer Royal Professor Sir Martin Rees says: 'It is not reasonable to think of humans as the end of anything.'

Theology since Darwin has been concerned with whether there is a fundamental difference between apes and human beings. Looking back through evolutionary history, is it possible to identify a point where human beings began: a moment when we became distinct from our animal ancestors? Now we need to project that question forward. Are we so sure that the embodied forms that we know today represent the zenith of evolution? Must a person be purely biological? When a human being and a machine combine, perhaps they produce something that is greater – something that we should regard as posthuman. We are at a stage in digital development where we need to ask whether we regard our current bodily form as a given … or whether we can develop it further, perhaps bring our humanness to fruition.

Increasingly we are able to use tools and devices of various kinds to improve on average physical abilities, to give some people – and it is always some, not all – enhanced powers. It's easy for us to be inconsistent about this. Take drugs for example. We admire athletes who go to immense lengths to improve their performance by a fraction of an inch or a tenth of a second, but we object when athletes use drugs to enhance their performance. And yet if I'm scheduled to give a lecture and I have a cold, I happily take medicine to get me through the day. What's the difference?

The difference is that a human being is a some*one*, not a some*thing*. Here's how you tell the difference. When two human beings get together, no matter how intimate they become or how close they feel, they remain two separate entities. When the book of Genesis says that two people can become one, it's expressing an aspiration, not a reality. In fact the tragedy of sex is that however much we want to be united with another person, we end up coming apart. Machines are different. If I link my mobile phone to a computer, and link that computer to your computer, then link them all

> A human being is a some*one*, not a some*thing*.

to the Internet, what we have created is effectively one big machine. My computer isn't aware that it is a separate piece of equipment. It doesn't feel sad because it can't get closer to the Internet. It just joins its computing power to whatever I connect it to. Humans, on the other hand, always remain separate units. My skin stops me from combining with you to become one unit.

So we can say that

1 human being + 1 human being = 2 human beings
but
1 computer + 1 computer = 1 bigger computer

But what about 1 human being + 1 computer. What does that make? The American cultural thinker Mark Poster believed that when a human and a machine (specifically a computer) work together, they become a new thing. He called it a *humachine*.

Most digital technology is designed to be used at very close range. A smart phone fits in the palm of your hand. A computer nestles on your lap or sits on a desk just a few inches away from you, meeting you at eye level. In either case, the screen addresses you from a place that is closer than most human beings ever will. An earpiece or headphones may come even closer, effectively shutting out other sounds. In future, technology that is wearable or implanted may come closer still. We carry our technology inside our intimate space, in breast pockets or tucked into our jeans, the territory that is usually reserved for lovers, children or pets. For many people it already seems normal to take a digital device to bed with them; indeed, research has shown that teenagers and some adults can experience anxiety if they are separated from their devices. The physical and psychological nearness of our devices is a sign of the unsparing relationship we have chosen to have with our digital representations. Can we, will we, should we, go a small step further, and become hu-machines?

In 1957 the biologist Julian Huxley wrote an essay in which he coined the word 'transhumanism'. He suggested that it might apply to an endeavour for the whole of humanity. With a slightly sarcastic nod to Jesus, he called his book *New Bottles for New Wine*. Perhaps, he said, the human body as we know it is not the best version that is available. Maybe we can improve. Why not build a better human? Indeed, since human beings are the first and only species to understand the full scope of evolution, do we not have a moral obligation to direct its future course?

To some extent this has always been true. When a Stone Age man made a flint axe, he was combining his own strength with a tool to give him an advantage over the next guy. The ethical question is what he does with the power this gives him. In the twenty-first century the stakes get much higher. If you have access to a computer and a broadband connection, while someone else doesn't, you have a huge power advantage over them, because as we know, information is power. And if you think that owning a computer is powerful, just imagine the degree of power that you can exercise if you own a social network like Facebook, or a search engine like Google, or an Internet Service Provider. Lots of questions arise about how we act justly and distribute power in a digital age, but I want to take us back to the human body, and the things we can do to improve its powers.

When you use a tool, whether it's a pair of glasses or a hammer or a computer, you act in some way on your environment. You change something. At the same time, as the sociologist Marshall McLuhan pointed out in the 1970s, the tool you are using acts on you. It changes you. Think of the ways we use mobile phones. Mobiles have massively changed the things we can do, and in turn, we have been changed by them. We do things differently because of mobile phones.

It's part of being human to want to overcome our limitations. We want to stay alive longer, transcend our humanity and eventually become God. We want to know more than our parents did. We want to see more than the naked eye can

> It's part of being human to want to overcome our limitations.

see. And we've always done things to enable this to happen. We've used drugs to enhance our sensations and awareness. We've tamed animals – like the horse for instance – to make us go faster and further. We've created personal devices to overcome our limitations – the hearing aid, spectacles, the heart pacemaker. We've built machines to extend what our bodies can do – from the wheel to the space rocket. Why not just continue this progress? If this makes you feel nervous, Huxley might say, just get over it! In every age some human beings have said that they can accept progress thus far, but resist it going further! Maybe biology itself is just one phase of human development. Maybe in the future our digital great-great-grandchildren will look at us with our organic, analogue bodies and smile at how charming and naive and limited we seem.

Perhaps you think I'm straying into science fiction here, but we can't just bury our heads in the sand. Tomorrow is almost here. My grandfather, who I remember very well, was born before the invention of the computer, the aeroplane and television. If he could see me now, typing into a computer, this might well look like science fiction to him. The future arrives very fast indeed. We get to make decisions about it, but we need to make them quickly. The question I started with, about the spectacles and the contact lenses and the eyeball-camera, was essentially asking this – what, if any, are the proper limits to human improvement?

Huxley's idea of transhumanism has become a kind of religion, and like most religions it has taken off in several different directions at once. Some transhumanists believe that if we take a 'hands-off' approach, human beings will simply keep on evolving without any particular help until they have gone far beyond what we now know. Bodies will just naturally carry on getting stronger and smarter as they have throughout history. Others believe that we can and should be much more proactive in upgrading the human body; we should actively create Artificial Intelligence and attach it or implant it in our bodies. As I suggested in our thought experiment at the start of this section, we already have quite a high tolerance of combining our bodies with gadgets, drugs and equipment to improve our everyday functionality. What is to stop us attaching or implanting computers and other machines, until you can't say what is a human and what is a machine? Many people already wear a device on their wrist that monitors their heart rate and oxygen levels and counts the number of steps they have taken that day. What would be the big deal about having such a device installed under your skin instead of wearing it on top of it? It's a short step from adding a piece of kit that enables you to do something better, to adjusting the body you were born with. It is increasingly possible to manipulate and combine human DNA to fix what we regard as disabilities, or to create humans with greater capacities than we know now.

When Professor Stephen Hawking died in 2018 the world lost one of its most brilliant scientists. If we could have uploaded Stephen Hawking's brain into a computer so that it was available after his death, would it not have been right to do so? Come to think of it, what about *my* brain? You wouldn't want that to be lost to the world, with all its hours of thinking and experience, just because my heart gives out. Why not be on the safe side and upload the contents of my brain into a global database? Even better, if we combine Stephen Hawking's brain with mine, and yours too, and lots of other people's brains, we would have a mega-brain that would be more powerful than anything the world has ever seen. And that mega-brain would be smart enough to create more mega-brains, and combine with them … and they would hook up with more brains until we ended up with one super-intelligence that was more powerful than all of the human brains in the world put together. Maybe it would be even more powerful than God. Suddenly I'm feeling breathless. I need to sit down for a while!

In 1965 the cryptologist I. J. Good coined a term for the point at which human development crosses over from being primarily biological to being primarily mechanical. He called it 'the Singularity'. The Singularity is a seamless blending of human intelligence and Artificial Intelligence and, at that point, technology becomes self-replicating. Good believed that human beings could create a machine that was ultra-intelligent, and that that ultra-intelligent machine could design even better machines, until there was an 'intelligence explosion' that would leave human beings far behind. Thus he said, 'The first ultra-intelligent machine is the last invention that man need ever make.' After that machines will take over and humans can stand down from their role as top dogs on Planet Earth. Many people who think about technology believe that there will come a point when machines become self-replicating in this way. When the Singularity occurs, they say, human beings will be redundant. Pretty soon we will become extinct – just a curious exhibit from the past, displayed in some museum of pre-digital technology.

When we start to think about the Singularity, or about improving the human body with technology, or combining individual humans into a greater whole, we pretty soon find ourselves asking religious questions about what it means to be a created being and what are the limits of our own creativity. God is creator, but are we not co-creators with him? We Christians are all about overcoming death, aren't we?

OK, let's leave aside the question of whether the Singularity is going to happen sooner or later or not at all. Let's focus instead on the big ethical questions that arise from the combination of organic human bodies and machines. What will happen if we lose the distinction between some*one* and some*thing*? Christians and many others have always taken a dim view of instrumentalizing the human body – seeing it as a means to an end. There is some sense in which human beings are designed by God and endowed with God's image, and that it should only ever be God's business, not ours, to change them, but this idea is changing in our culture. The growing popularity of tattoos, prosthetics and body modification is just one of the signs of that. We are increasingly comfortable to blur the boundary between human and artefact; to see the human body as not much more than raw material out of which we can construct something to our taste. That's what Mary Shelley was writing about in her book *Frankenstein* two hundred years ago. How will we decide what is a good modification and what is a bad one? For instance, if we can manipulate genes so that human beings are not born with disabilities, should we do that? What if we went further? If a given gender

> We are increasingly comfortable to see the human body as not much more than raw material.

or race is associated with disadvantage, why not eliminate it altogether? At what point, if any, should we say: 'That's far enough'? And how in practice could we do that?

The trouble is, if human beings are no longer a single species, because some have been modified in one direction and some in another, we will be powerless to prevent a growing division between one type of human being and another. Already there's a risk of a growing division between technology-rich and technology-poor – a kind of technological apartheid. What if there was a parallel 'genetic divide', with some humans genetically adapted for high-grade lives and others genetically adapted for lives of service? In fact, that divide already seems to exist massively in the world, and we don't seem to do much about it. The more I think about it, the more issues of transhumanism seem pretty close to the ethical issues of our own time.

What Next?

As with all new technologies, we have choices to make. If it's any comfort, we've been here before – or at least somewhere a bit like it. In 1921, when public broadcasting became available for the first time, very few people had any idea what challenges and opportunities it was going to throw up. At first it was assumed that the primary purpose of broadcasting was commercial, but soon a handful of young men led by a railway engineer called John Reith began to think through what else the new medium could do, and what it was for. Though these pioneers were almost exclusively Christians, they were driven by a liberal secular vision that the new medium should enhance human wellbeing. Through the early years of broadcasting they developed what became known as the Reithian doctrine. It said that broadcasting had a social purpose and not merely a commercial one. It said that broadcasting should be conducted according to a set of values that were truthful and not exploitative. It said that the artistic and technical qualities of production should be as high as possible. It said that the raison d'être of broadcasting was to inform, educate and entertain. These values were sometimes ignored and never codified, but they have profoundly shaped the culture of the broadcasting era.

> As with all new technologies, we have choices to make.

The first digital era is throwing up challenges and

opportunities that are at least as great as those of 1922. It's easy to think that what we're dealing with is just new technology that's creating new possibilities, but the fundamentally important issues are not about digital technology and what we can do with it, but about digital culture and what it will do to us.

Robots everywhere

My father worked in the same insurance company for almost 40 years. He was a clerk, keeping records in ledgers and making calculations, and arranging business on the phone, sometimes using his schoolboy French to talk to his opposite number in Paris. The work that he did for all those years, that paid for my school uniform and summer holidays, is probably now just a few lines of a code in a computer somewhere. In digital culture, work is changing rapidly. Probably the first robot to directly take over the role of a human being in the workplace was Unimate. Unimate was created by an engineer called Joseph Engelberger and an entrepreneur called George Devol, and it started work in 1961, which happens to be the same year that I was born. The robot arm was installed on the General Motors assembly line, where it performed simple, repetitive tasks like extracting die-castings from machines and performing spot welding on vehicles. Those were tasks that had previously been performed by human beings, who laughed and swapped cigarettes on the line, and were paid on a Friday night, and took money home to their families. Unimate was just the first of a thousand million robots to join the workplace, forcing a thousand million people to find a new mode of existence. Supermarket checkout staff, delivery drivers, call centre operators and bookkeepers – all these people and many more are likely to see their jobs disappear over the next couple of decades at the most. Many of the jobs that will disappear are boring, repetitive or dangerous, but as well as contributing to the economy, work gives a sense of purpose to individuals, and often provides a community of belonging. When that is gone, what will replace it? Presumably new jobs will emerge, as they usually do when technology disrupts the economy, but there may well be many years of turbulence and many social and emotional casualties in the first digital age. There will also be a concentration of power and wealth in the hands of those who control the machinery and possess knowledge, just as there was in the Industrial Revolution. That's already well under way. If the great need of the coming generation is going to be for purpose and creative occupation, the Church, which understands itself as having an insight into God's purpose for the world, could well have a vital role to play. To achieve this it will need to lift its eyes from its own survival, and its internal politics, and become a true servant to the community.

Education is another sphere where digital technology is likely to play a huge role. One of the great dilemmas faced by classroom teachers, for example, is the difficulty of tailoring learning to the needs of each individual child. It is almost impossible for a teacher with a class of thirty or more children to know exactly what each child has learnt and understood, when they need to be challenged, and when they need extra help. Robots are great at this. A computer can 'get to know' each individual child, testing them on what they have understood, recording what they know and explaining what they need to learn. A computer is a vastly more efficient maths teacher than a human being. It is also less expensive to maintain than a flesh-and-blood teacher, can differentiate between the needs of students, and doesn't need to take holidays. On the other hand, a computer can't listen sympathetically and patiently to a child's needs. It can't say, 'I'm sorry your cat died.' A computer can't say, 'I felt like that once, but I got over it.' It can't encourage a child to reach for the stars or find yet another fun new way to explain long division. The likelihood is that the role of the teacher as mentor will grow, and their role as a dispenser of facts and methodology will diminish. In the nineteenth century, churches invented the Sunday School as a way of helping the poorest children to thrive. What role will they discover in the twenty-first century to help adults and children grow as human beings and as digital citizens? Can they ensure that digital education is available to children whatever their parents' resources? Will they be able to lead by example, even though most churches still see the business of learning faith as derivative from Higher Education, with a qualified pastor giving a weekly mini-lecture from the pulpit? Will Christians in the next generation be able to learn and interrogate the facts of their faith in other ways, while pastors become mentors and encouragers, relying on their character and their faith experience rather than their theological training and their status in the church as their core qualification?

Healthcare is another area that is already being transformed by digital culture. Radiologists scan hundreds of mammogram images for early signs of breast cancer. Their work is vital in diagnosing and treating sufferers. It takes years to train a radiologist to interpret these images, and the results are highly accurate, though not perfect of course. Now though, computers with Artificial Intelligence have been programmed to analyse mammograms. They can work much faster than human radiographers and achieve the same level of accuracy. As time goes by, digital analysis will inevitably overtake human input. Diagnosis will be speeded up and treatment will be improved, but a crucial medical discipline will be lost or transformed. One of the projects working in this area is IBM's super-computer Watson. Watson is a question-answering system not unlike domestic servants such as Siri or Alexa. Watson's first outing wasn't in healthcare at all, but in an episode of the US TV gameshow *Jeopardy!* Playing the quiz against two former champions, Watson used its voice-recognition technology to interpret the questions put to it and drew on its four terabytes of information to deliver the answers. Watson won every round, and would have walked away with the $1 million prize, except that it didn't have any legs. Playing *Jeopardy!* was only ever meant to be a light-hearted test-run for Watson. Its primary function is to collect and sift vast amounts of medical research and make them accessible to doctors. For example, it has access to the databases of 1000 of the world's top oncologists, meaning that it can diagnose cancer with greater accuracy than any single doctor in history ever has. It provides patients and physicians with personalized, evidence-based diagnoses and treatment recommendations. There's no reason why there shouldn't be a terminal with access to Watson in every GP surgery in the world – no reason that is except the commercial one, that someone has to pay for it.

Digital technology is also responsible for the development of personalized medicine. In the past, most treatments have relied on the experience of the doctor, who has studied diseases like yours, and can draw on the experience of others who have treated similar patients. What the doctor couldn't do is to prescribe the perfect treatment for you as an individual. In the near future, though, it will be possible to use digital diagnostics to analyse your own unique situation and prescribe a treatment or even a medicine tailored exclusively for you. For a few pounds it is possible to read your entire genetic sequence and analyse precisely what intervention you need to achieve the results you want.

Medicine, which has always been a science of averages, is becoming a precise art.

Of course there are a number of problems with this. As is the case with most new technologies, the people likely to benefit in the first instance are those who can afford to pay for such specialized diagnosis and treatment. Those who can't afford it will have to fall back on less reliable methods. In many parts of the world, healthcare is paid for by an insurance system. Now that the cost of analysing an individual's genetic make-up has dropped below the cost of a few months' insurance, it is likely that insurance companies are going to want to see your genetic passport before they agree to cover you. If they discover that you have a disposition to cancer or heart disease or sickle cell, they will raise your insurance premiums accordingly. People who, through no fault of their own, are likely to need expensive medical care may find that it is unaffordable. Combine this with the lifestyle information that has been extracted from your supermarket or your bank, and you may find that people who smoke, or drink alcohol, or eat unhealthily or drive too fast will be 'punished' by higher premiums, if they can get insurance at all. Once again, digital technology is likely to drive a wedge between rich and poor. Those who are powerful or comfortable in the analogue era will be more so in the digital era. In the nineteenth century, Christians were at the forefront of making sure that the best healthcare was available to people who couldn't pay for it themselves. Will Christians once again be at the forefront of ensuring justice in the digital world?

> Digital technology is likely to drive a wedge between rich and poor.

Although I said earlier that the Internet emerged in the 1980s, it had an earlier history. The system of conveying packets of information between networked computers in digital form can be dated back to the late 1960s. The first application was called the Arpanet, and it was developed in California using funding provided by the US military. Fifty years later, weapons are still a major area of digital research and development. In a high-tech control centre in a remote part of East Anglia, pilots from the RAF sit in front of flickering computer screens. They are controlling Unmanned Aerial Vehicles (commonly known as drones) flying over Afghanistan, ten thousand miles away. The drones cost £10 million each, and they are equipped with surveillance cameras to watch for Taliban fighters. They can also be equipped with Hellfire missiles and laser-guided bombs. The military claims that they can pinpoint their targets with great accuracy, and that may be true. Remote controlled weapons are the future of modern warfare. Robotic soldiers are being developed and may soon fight alongside augmented human soldiers or else replace humans on the battlefield altogether. Will they be able to distinguish targets accurately and use force proportionately? Does it even make sense to talk about proportionality in warfare, when one side has a huge technological advantage?

Digital technology has the potential to help the human race with many of the critical problems we are facing today. Technology is vital to research that is tackling major diseases. It could help us deal with global food shortages and even to tackle global warming, but all of this depends on how we manage it. We are now into the second and third generation of digitally enabled humanity, but it still isn't clear who will give us a lead in thinking through the fundamental questions about its impact. Whose job is it to manage all of this? Politicians might be able to take a lead, but we will need to recognize that, just as with pressing issues around climate change, many of the possibilities and problems raised by digital culture are supra-national, so solutions that prioritize the power of individual states aren't going to work. Religious figures such as popes, bishops and ayatollahs may not help much either, since their focus in the twenty-first century is mostly on the survival of their own cultures. In the values vacuum that has been left, technology companies and their leaders have taken the lead in shaping a digital morality for the future. I know from personal contact that many of them suffer from a sort of vertigo, realizing what enormous changes are coming in on the digital tidal wave, but ill-equipped to manage their social and cultural impact. Individual tech users in our billions mostly accept the technology that is marketed to us, without stopping to question what it means or where it is leading.

There are some things that cannot be expressed digitally – mystery, empathy, purpose, creativity, love, God. These are some of the most fundamental dimensions of being human. The challenge for Christians in each new generation is to work out what our faith means in the cultural

> There are some things that cannot be expressed digitally – mystery, empathy, purpose, creativity, love, God.

space in which we find ourselves. Surely we can never have too much information. But too little understanding – that's another thing.

Glossary

Algorithm   A part of a computer program that has been designed to solve a problem or answer a specific set of questions.

Application, app   A computer program designed to perform a specific task.

Artificial intelligence (AI)   A loose term to describe the ability of computers or other machines to solve problems using the sort of intelligence usually displayed by humans. Weak AI describes the ability of computers to perform complex but straightforward tasks, such as playing chess or operating an assembly line. Strong AI describes the ability of a computer to 'learn' from its own experience to such a degree that it is able to deal with situations it has not encountered before.

Augmented reality   An enhanced view of reality, produced by overlaying digital information onto the user's own experience, often using adapted lenses. For example, a user wearing Augmented reality glasses might look at another person, and be offered additional information about them, such as their name, age, gender, wealth or past history.

Avatar   A graphic image used by an individual to represent themselves online, for example in a computer game or a chat room. A user can often choose or design their own avatar, which may or may not share their looks or personality. The word avatar is originally used for the incarnation of a Hindu God.

Bot   A bot (or web bot) is a piece of software that runs automated tasks on the Internet. A bot can work much faster than a human operator, and once set off on its task it needs no human supervision. Typically a bot is used for 'spidering', i.e. crawling through web pages to collect and analyse information. Bots constitute more than half of all the traffic on the World Wide Web.

Clicktivism   Clicktivism is a contraction of the words click and activism. It describes the use of the Internet for political or social action such as petitions, open letters and protests. It is sometimes suggested that clicktivism is a 'cheap' form of social engagement with little real commitment. Some websites use petitions to gather commercially useful information about users.

Cloud, The   Another word for the Internet. The Cloud is often associated with the centralized storage of information or programs that can be accessed from any computer terminal.

Crowdsourcing   Crowdsourcing is using the Internet to locate and attract large numbers of people to participate in a project or deliver an outcome. It may be used to collect funding or sponsorship, e.g. to finance a work of art or a company start-up. It can also be used to engage large numbers of people in scientific research or opinion polling. Crowdsourcing can be used to access the wisdom of the hive mind.

Cyberspace The intangible territory in which digital information is transmitted through networks of computers. The term was coined by William Gibson in his 1984 book, Neuromancer. He later dismissed it as meaningless, but it remains useful as a metaphor for the imagined world of disembodied information.

Cyborg A contraction of the words cybernetic and organism. A cyborg is a being that is part-human and part-machine: a combination of the biological elements of a human body with added technological components. A person with a heart pacemaker or cochlear implant could be considered a cyborg, but it is more often used to describe a person, either in science fiction or in Real Life, whose enhancement has given them super-human powers.

Deep web, dark web The deep web (or deep net) is that part of the World Wide Web that is not accessible to normal web browsers. It can only be accessed by specialist software that is not readily available. The dark web refers to those parts of the deep web that are used for secretive, immoral or criminal activities such as extreme pornography or espionage.

Digital, digitize, digitization Digital information is data that is stored, recorded or transmitted as a sequence of 1s and 0s. The presence or absence of small, fast-moving electronic bits is used to turn information of many kinds into long strings of code. This is the process of digitization. These signals carry instructions within a machine. Digital data has no meaning of itself, until it has been decoded and turned back into sounds, images or information that can be recognized by humans.

Email A system of sending and receiving messages via the

Internet. Email servers receive, store and deliver messages on behalf of clients.

Emoji Emojis are graphic symbols designed for transmission in mobile phone or other digital messaging. They constitute a pictorial language, with upwards of 3,000 symbols currently available. Emojis are created by large Internet companies such as Apple, but their meaning is defined by users. Originating in Japan, the word is a combination of e- (meaning picture) and -moji (meaning character.)

Emoticon An emoticon is a sequence of letters or punctuation marks combined to represent a human face showing an emotion, for example :-) for smiling. Emoticons emerged in the early days of digital communication as a simple way of conveying feelings in a few characters.

Global Positioning System (GPS) GPS is a system that uses satellites to determine a location on the earth's surface. Regular signals are transmitted by 24 satellites in constant orbit about 12,000 miles above the earth's surface. A GPS receiver on earth collects signals from three or more satellites. By determining the length of time it has taken for each signal to reach the receiver, it can triangulate a location (known as a geolocation) with an accuracy within a few metres. The system is owned by the United States government and managed by the US Air Force. It has many uses, including satellite navigation in cars and the targeting of missile strikes.

Haptic technology Haptic technology uses digital information to imitate and relay the sensation of touch and movement. It can refer to means of controlling computers or phones by touching and swiping, as opposed to typing instructions via a keyboard. It can also refer to the synthesizing of human touch using digital signals to transmit information.

Hive mind The hive mind refers to the collective wisdom of a large community of people, typically accessed through the Internet. The term refers to the behaviour of a swarm of bees working together to achieve a single purpose. It is sometimes used positively, for instance when seeking a consensus from a large number of people for a difficult decision. It is sometimes used negatively, as when a large number of people set aside their individual wisdom to go with the will of the crowd.

Internet The Internet is a global system of interconnected networks passing digital information around the world through high-speed fibre-optic cables. These cables are connected through major physical hubs around the world. It is loosely governed by major companies cooperating on issues such as Internet Protocol addresses (IP addresses) and Domain Names. There is at present only one publicly available Internet, though of course governments and commercial interests are able to build and employ their own networks.

Internet Service Provider (ISP) An Internet Service Provider is a company that sells Internet access to individuals, providing the final link between the Internet and an individual house or business address.

IP address (Internet Protocol address) Every device connected to the Internet, whether it is a laptop computer or a smart phone, has a unique IP address. It takes the form of a numerical code, and acts like the address of a building, enabling networks to deliver information to the right place. It can be expressed as a series of numbers, such as 172.16.244.1, or as a series of 32 1s and 0s.

Multi-User Domain (MUD)   A computer program that allows multiple users to interact with each other online, typically to play games. It may take the form of an imagined virtual world in which users adopt avatars and play roles. Sometimes large numbers of participants can take part in Massively Multi-Player Online Role-playing Games, known as MMORPGs. An online church is a form of Multi-User Domain.

Net neutrality   Net neutrality is the principle that Internet Service Providers should deliver all information with equal priority and speed and without discrimination, irrespective of who has provided or requested that information.

Offline   Offline may refer to a computer that is operating while disconnected from the Internet. It is also sometimes used as a generic term to refer to life and relationships in organic or physical space.

Online   Connected to the Internet or another computer network.

Pixel   Short for picture element, a pixel is a tiny point of light of a single colour on a computer screen. Many thousands of pixels combine like jigsaw pieces to make up a whole image.

Real Life   Real Life is commonly used for things that happen in the world of human senses, as opposed to the world made up of digital signals. It is a contested term, because many technologists would argue that even digital information has a physical form and is a constituent part of human and/or divine creation.

Robot A robot is a physical machine that is only capable of carrying out tasks automatically, according to the way it has been designed or programmed. Some robots are designed to look like humans, or to perform tasks that imitate humans. Such robots are sometimes referred to as android (if they look like males) or gynoid (if they look like females).

Screen name, username A screen name or username (or handle) is a word or series of letters used to represent an individual in a computer program.

Selfie A photograph, usually taken with a smart phone, in which the photographer appears at the centre of the action.

Singularity, the (or the Technological Singularity) An imagined moment in the future when computers have the capacity to develop and reproduce themselves without human intervention. At this point, technology is irreversible and beyond human control. It represents a fundamental change in the place of human beings in the created order – the end of the 'human era' in world history.

Smart phone A smart phone is a mobile device connected to the Internet that includes a facility to make voice calls.

Teledildonic A teledildonic is an Internet-linked sex toy that can be used by one or more people at the same time. Teledildonic (or cyberdildonic) describes a device connected to the Internet that is used for sexual stimulation of a partner who is also connected to the Internet, but in another location or time.

Turing Test In 1950 the computer scientist Alan Turing proposed an experiment in which a researcher hidden behind a screen had two conversations – one with a man and the other with a woman. He wanted to find out whether the researcher would always be able to tell which was which. Turing called this exercise 'the Imitation Game', but it is often known as the Turing Test. Turing wondered whether it would ever be possible to create a computer that could perform as well as, or better than, a human being at the Imitation Game. He proposed this as a test to judge whether machines could think for themselves.

Uncanny Valley   The Uncanny Valley is a term in robotics. It describes the discovery that human beings are increasingly attracted to robots as they become increasingly lifelike. However, there is a point at which the robot becomes so nearly indistinguishable from a human that the observer is 'spooked' and their emotional attraction is reversed. This observation was first made in 1970 by the Japanese Robotics professor Masahiro Mori.

Virtual reality   Virtual reality is the use of a computer to generate highly realistic and immersive environments. Typically, a human user is equipped with a headset that shows 3D images and hyper-realistic sounds, and where the image appears to move with the user. It has many applications, for instance in surgery, architecture and warfare.

Wiki   Any website that allows multiple writers and editors to contribute information to or receive information from a single source. Some wikis are open only to registered users, while others are open to the general public. Information is commonly published without prior editing, and users can change or refine it online.

Whole Brain Emulation (WBE)   Whole Brain Emulation is a technique not yet available, in which all of the information contained in a single human brain is either duplicated or uploaded into a computer.

World Wide Web (WWW)   The World Wide Web (or 'the web') is *not* the same as the Internet. It is a massive application that uses the Internet to allow individuals and communities to create and publish their own information in the form of websites. These sites are publicly available and can be accessed using a web browser. The World Wide Web was developed in the early 1990s by the English technologist Sir Tim Berners-Lee. It was his decision that the technology should be available free of charge to all who wished to use it.